T0210022

Easy
Chord Melody for Jazz Guitar

Carlos Brizzola

WestBow Press books may be ordered through booksellers or by contacting:

WestBow Press
A Division of Thomas Nelson & Zondervan
1663 Liberty Drive
Bloomington, IN 47403
www.westbowpress.com
1 (866) 928-1240

ISBN: 978-1-9736-3884-1 (sc)
ISBN: 978-1-9736-3883-4 (e)

Print information available on the last page.

WestBow Press rev. date: 09/10/2018

Easy Chord Melody For Jazz Guitar – Book 1

Index and Topics

Introduction.

Since I was a teenager, I was always enchanted by the finesse and talent of Joe Pass playing solos on his guitar.

I studied him for many years trying to figure it out. What on earth was Joe doing, and how did he manage to choose so well the chords and phrases to play?

After some time of playing and observing it finally dawned on me that the technique of Chord Melody is a mix of alternated chords and phrases put together; also, that the chords used are strategically picked where the top note of the chord, or the first voice, would match the note of the melody in that particular beat of the bar you're playing.

When I realized that, things become a bit more clearer in my mind and I started to combine different inversions of chords, for example, C major chord with the top note on the root (EGC), then with the top note on the 3rd (CGE) and finally with the top note on the 5th (CEG).

After that, I started to combine single notes in between chords, so I managed to create alternate melodies joining with the chords; in this way I was able to produce part of the melody by using a block of notes or chords and also single note melodic phrasing.

Suddenly I figured out that Chord Melody was real fun to play and was not that difficult. My guarantee is simply that if I can manage to see it by myself, anyone can do it. Maybe the problem is that there's not many manuals, guitar books or videos on the internet for us guitarists to consult and learn this subject; and more than that, the major part of guitar instructors, on the internet, who dare to discuss this subject, speak too much and play too little, so managing to make you tired and bored even before you start.

My objective here is to concentrate on the important parts of this concept, without wasting your precious time and energy; by putting you to play immediately, without thinking too much about it and approaching it as practically as possible, you will become more and more familiar with this technique, and by doing what I am asking you to do, will gradually increase and improve your chord vocabulary. In the near future you will associate the sounds of the chords and phrases, you are learning, with your own creativity, enabling you to play much better.

I strongly suggest from the start that you study every song, bar by bar, playing only the chords, making sure you get familiar with them. Then go for the phrases in between the chords gradually increasing extra bars to it and so on. Try to play it in a slow tempo and make sure all the notes involved are well played and sound correct. Do not hurry! Take your time and enjoy it.

There are other ways to master this technique which are more of a complex study on this subject, by using the music and jazz theories, but this is best left for another book.

If you perhaps need an audio backing track as a reference, email me and I will be more than happy to send you the mp3 files to help you with the studies, completely FREE of charge.

My email is: easychordmelody@gmail.com

also my website is: www.carlosbrizzola.com

Well let's start to work! I am sure you will not regret it.

Thanking you so much.

Carlos Brizzola

Easy
Chord Melody for Jazz Guitar
Book I

by Carlos Brizzola

Acknowledgements

This book is dedicated to my parents for encouraging me to learn music and play a musical instrument, and for showing me the right direction along this wonderful and mesmerizing path of sounds and notes. They did it with such love and enthusiasm by believing in what I was doing and always supporting me.

I still hearing my Mum singing "How Great Thou Art" and seeing my Dad showing me how to position my little fingers on the fret-board to play my first chords on the guitar.
It is because of my parents that I am here today and I will forever carry in my heart all the memories, all their gestures, both words and love.

"Mum and Dad, I love you so much. Here is the rewarded prize and honour for all you have done for me."

I want to say thank you to my dear friend Simona Mihai for believing in me and for your lovely support and encouragement on this project.

Also a special thanks to Peter Levy who so kindly revised all the text in this book.

Harmonized Major Scale Voicing

study designed by Carlos Brizzola

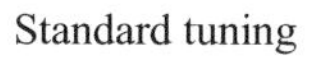

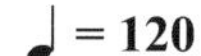

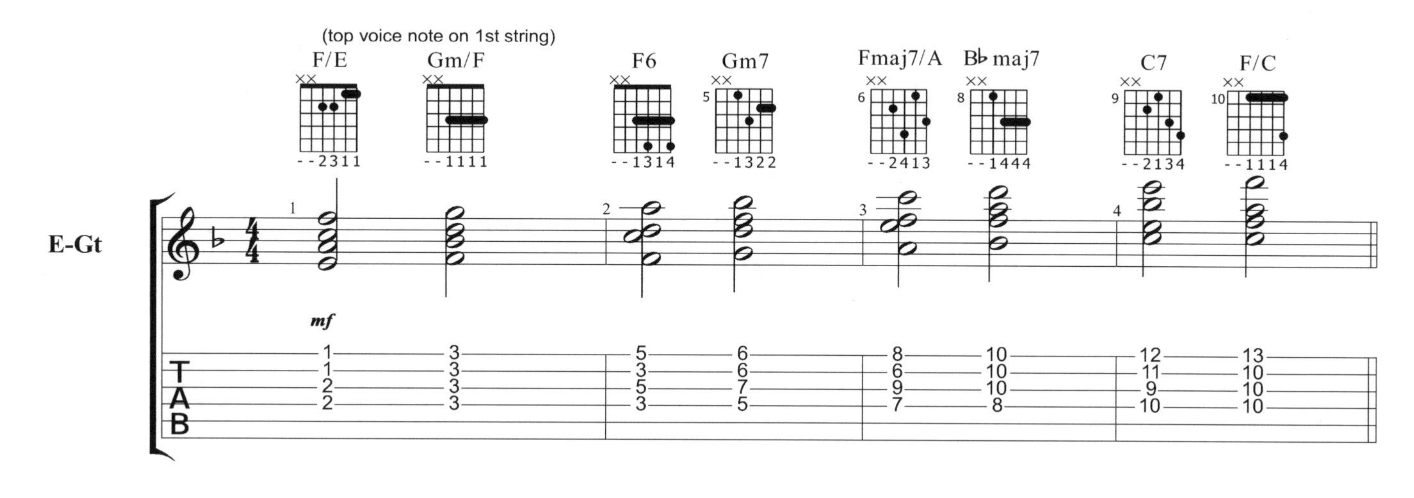

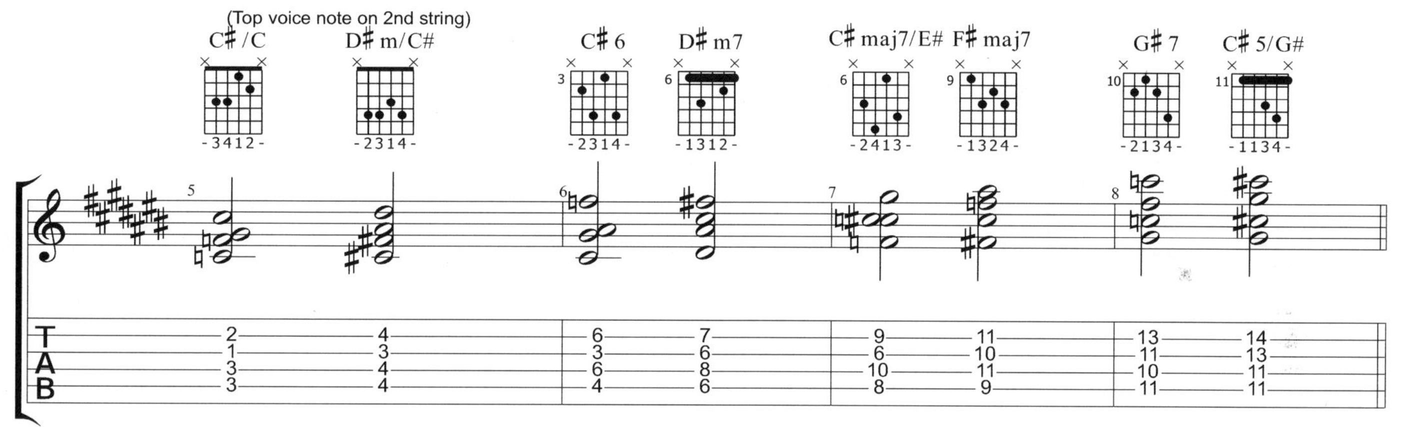

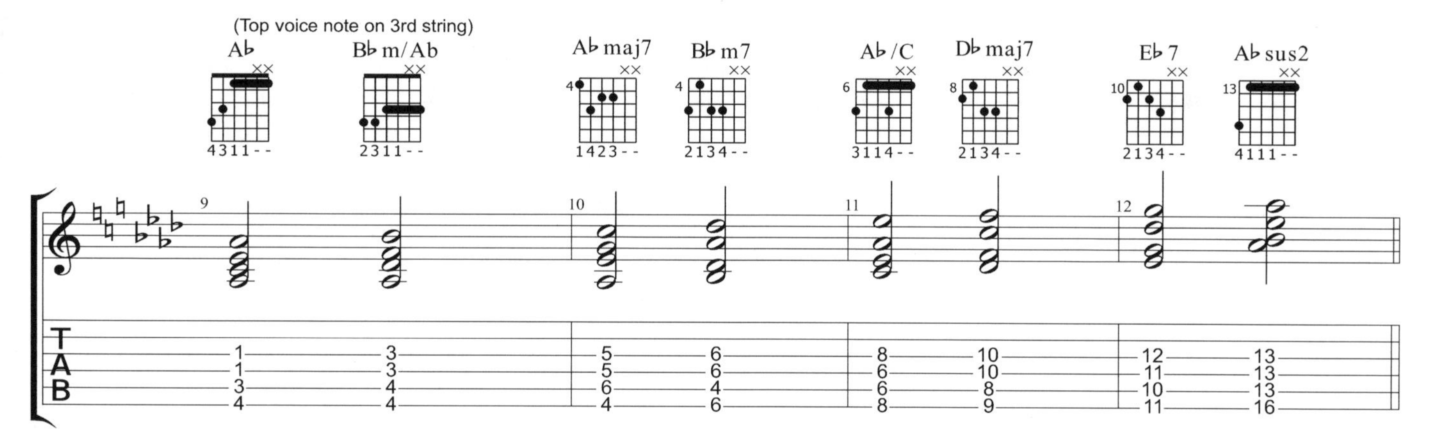

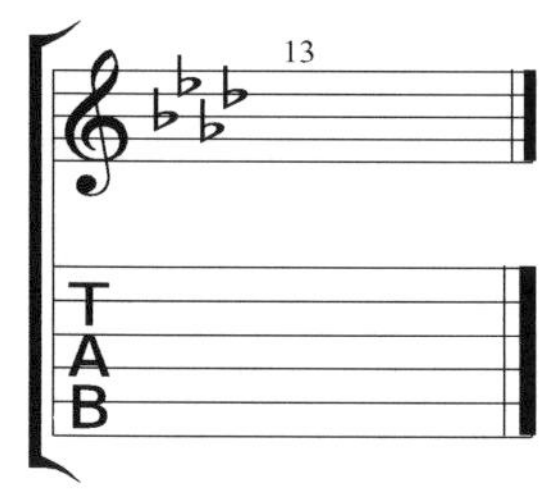

Harmonized Minor Scale Voicing

study designed by Carlos Brizzola

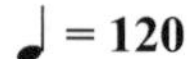

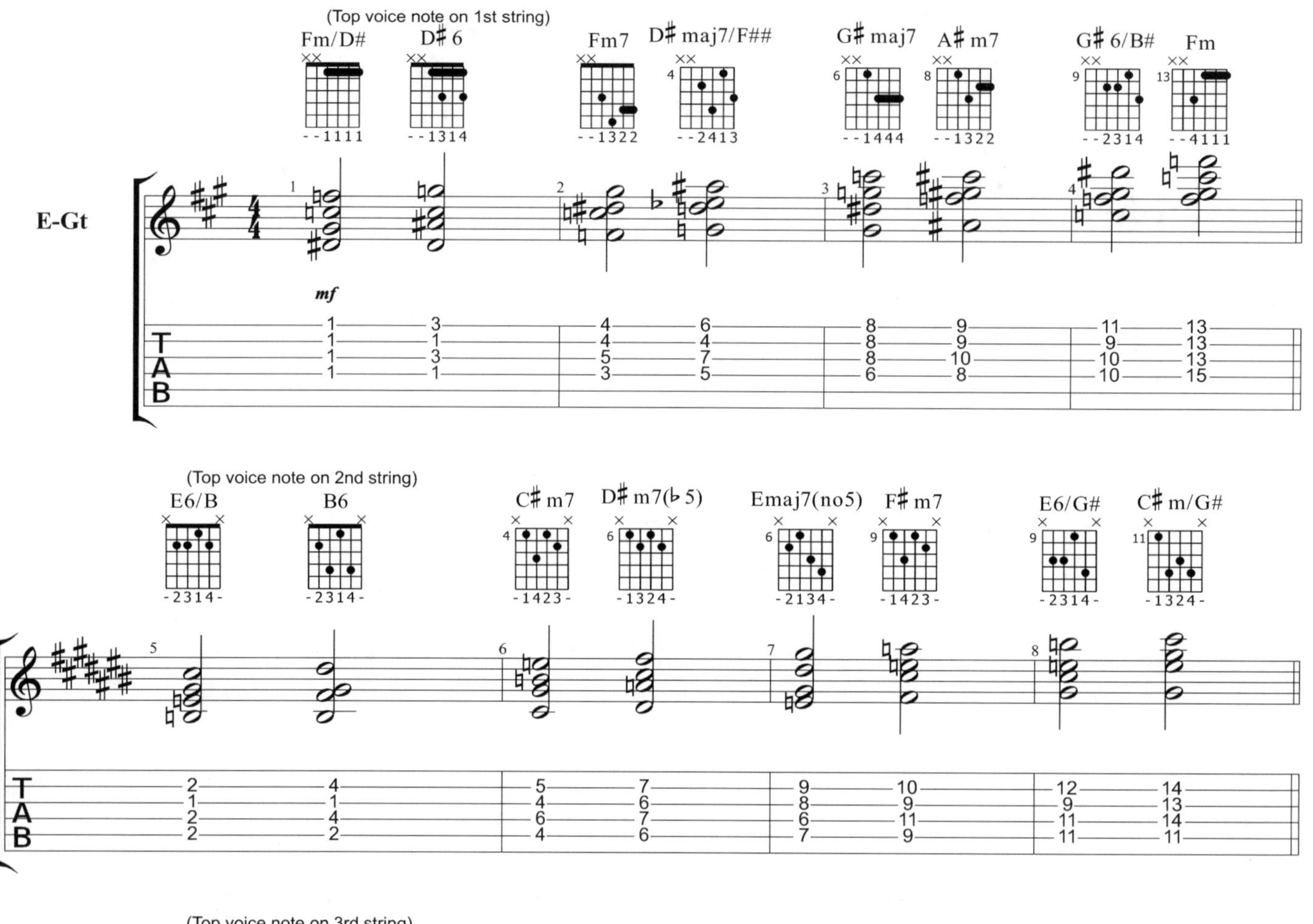

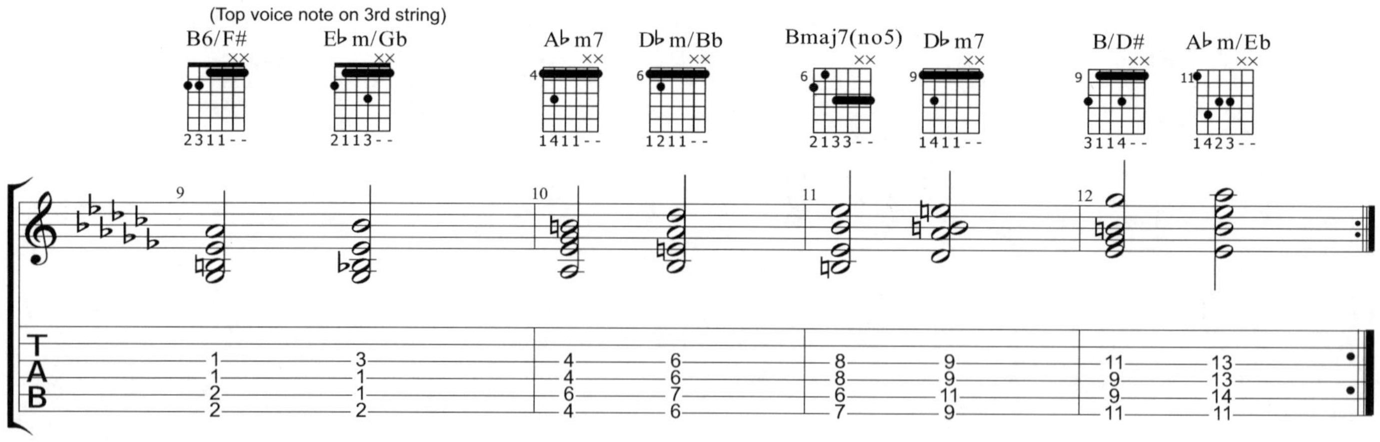

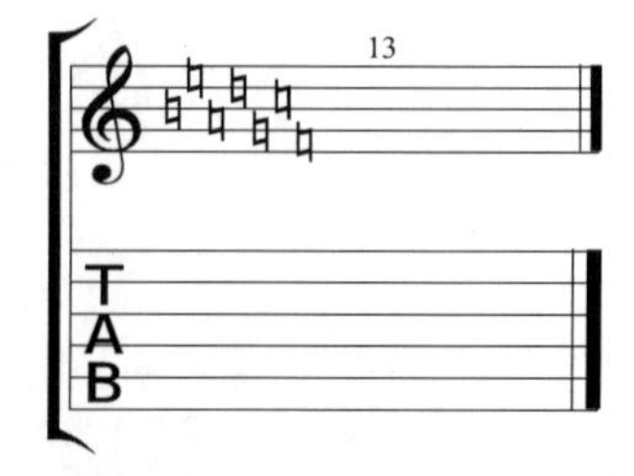

Harmonized Dominant Scale Voicing

study designed by Carlos Brizzola

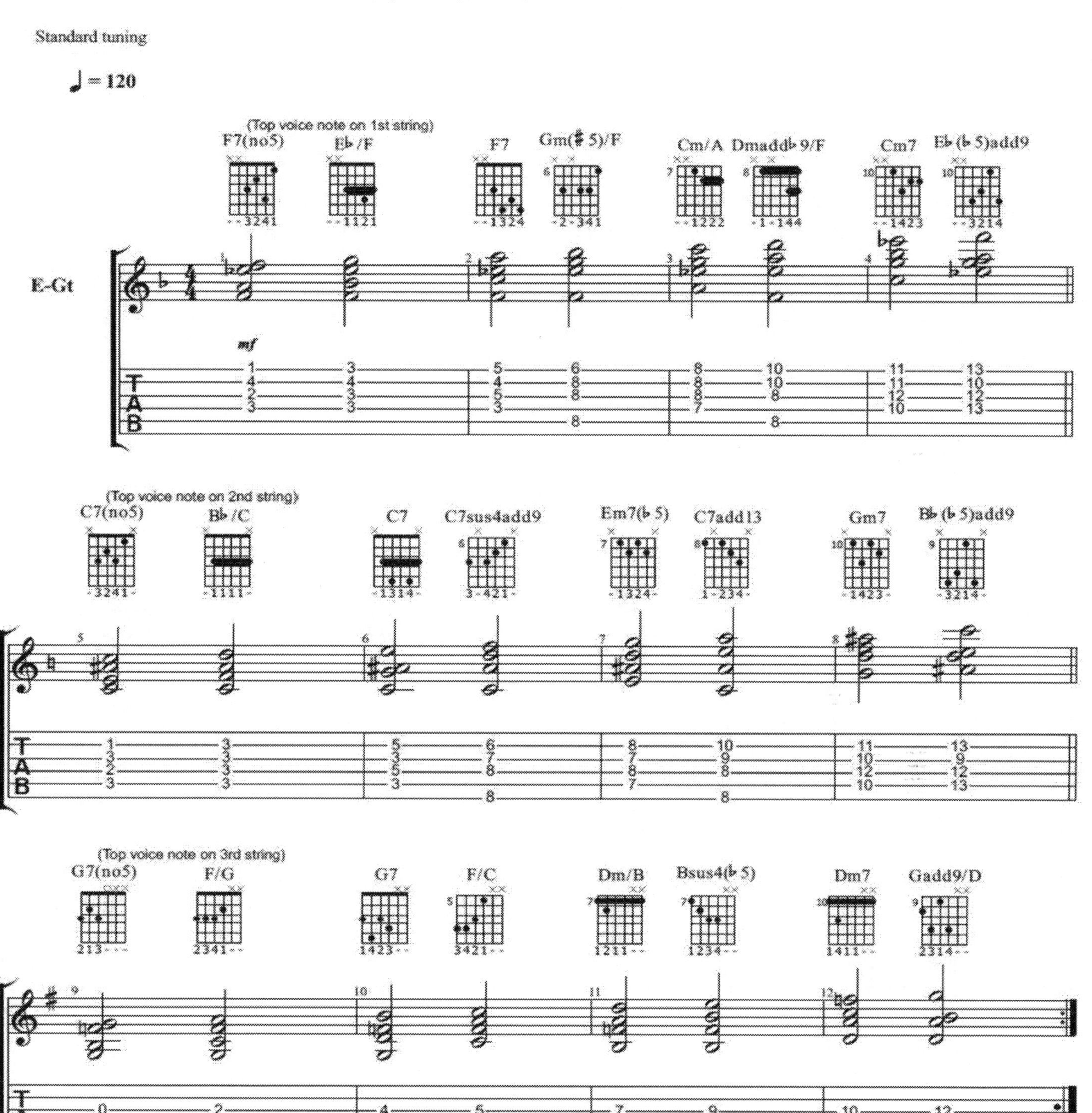

Harmonized Dorian Mode Voicing

study designed by Carlos Brizzola

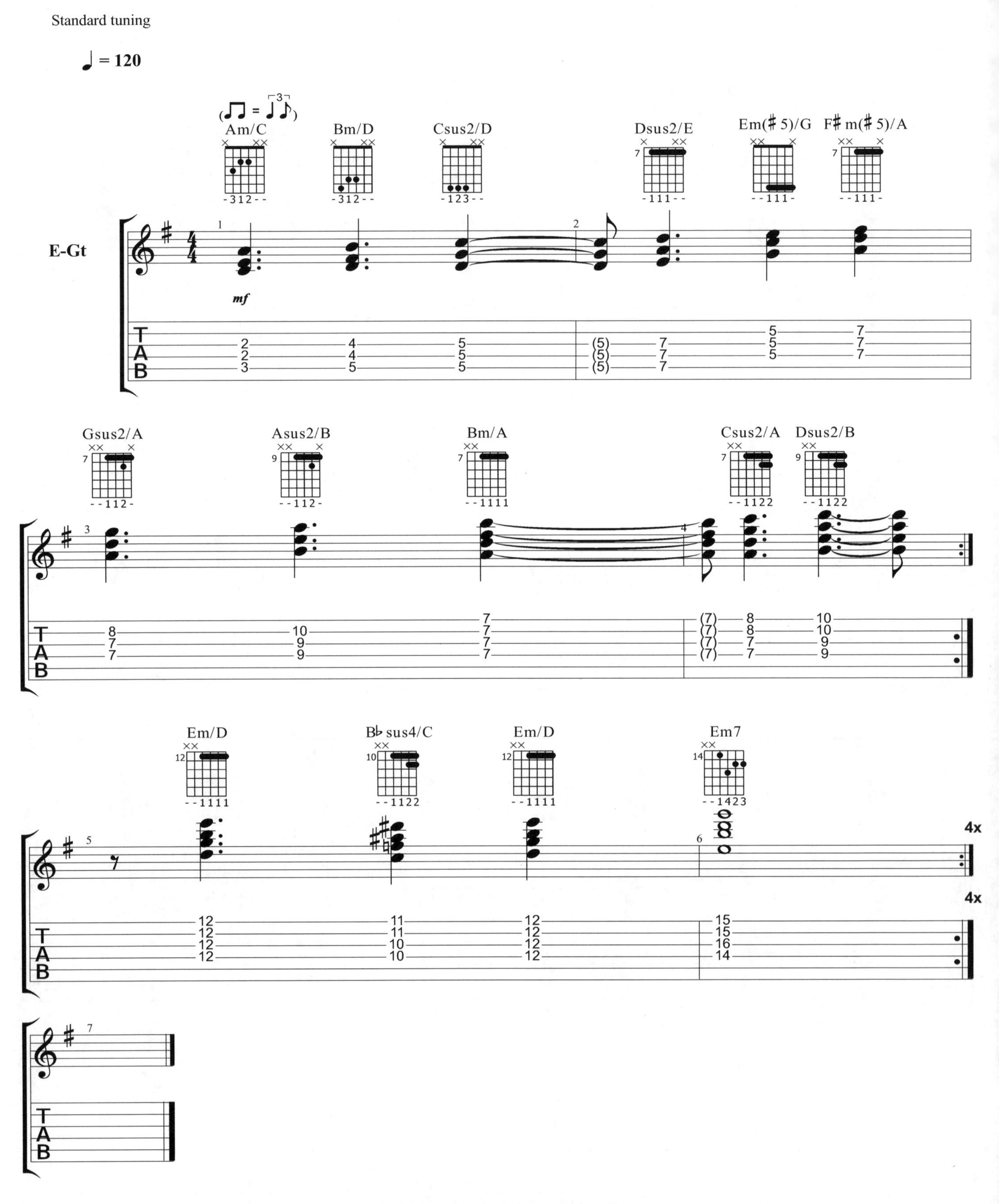

Harmonized Bebop Locrian Scale Voicing

study designed by Carlos Brizzola

Em7(♭5)
A7add♭13
Aaug/G
Dm9
Bebop Locrian Scale

Harmonized Major Pentatonic Scale

study designed by Carlos Brizzola

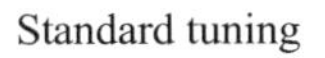

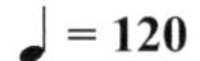

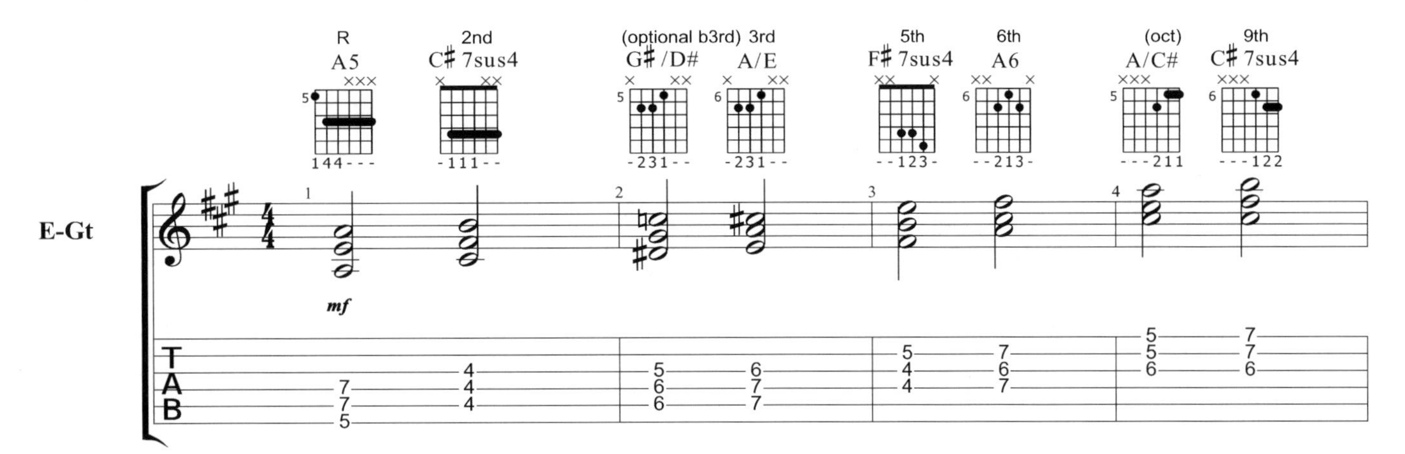

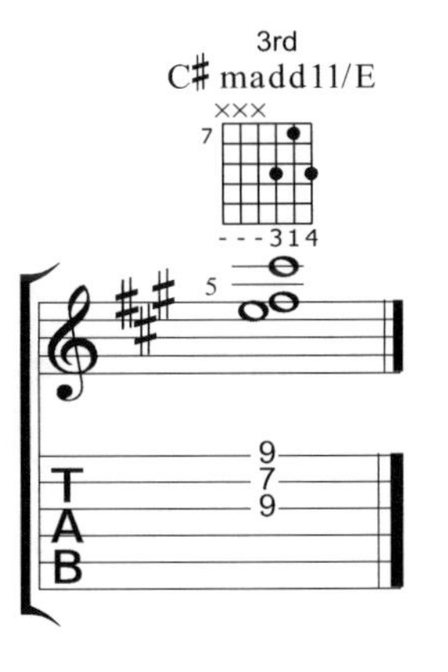

Harmonized Minor Pentatonic Scale

study designed by Carlos Brizzola

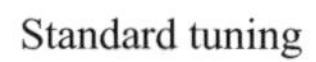

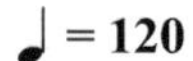

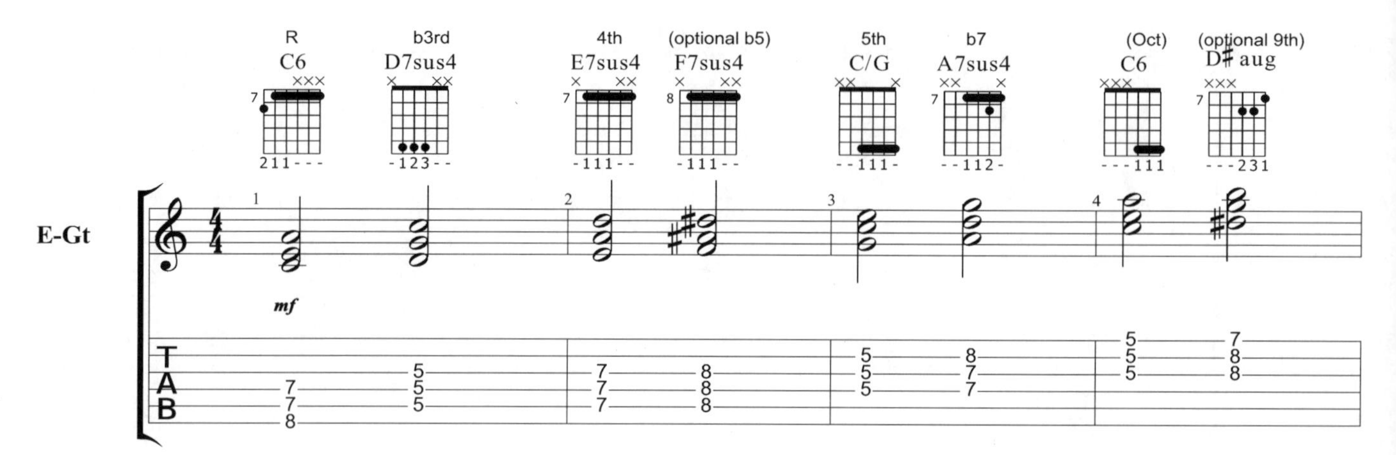

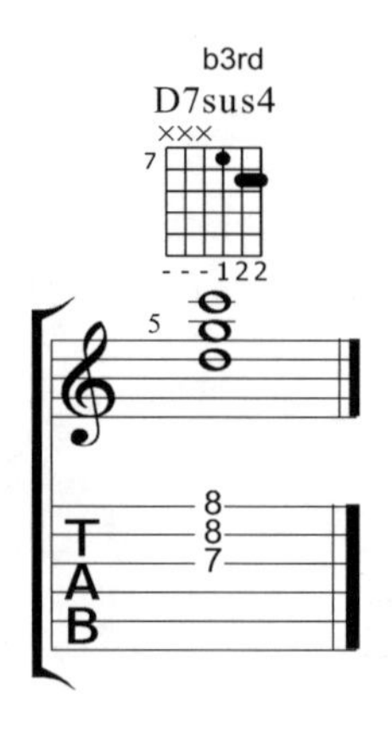

Chromatic Movement Over Major Scale

study designed by Carlos Brizzola

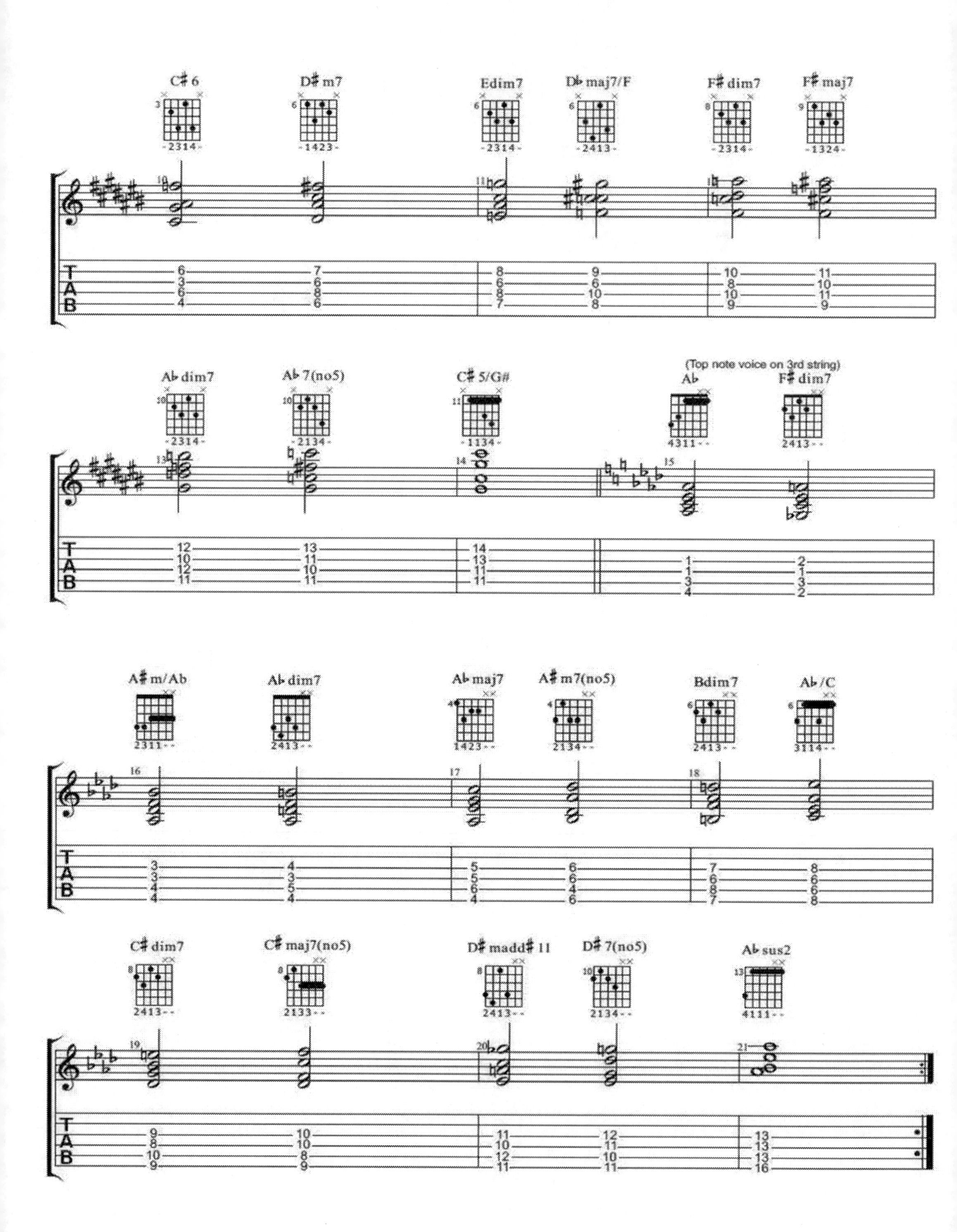
C♯6
D♯m7
Edim7
D♭maj7/F
F♯dim7
F♯maj7
A♭dim7
A♭7(no5)
C♯5/G♯
(Top note voice on 3rd string)
A♭
F♯dim7
A♯m/Ab
A♭dim7
A♭maj7
A♯m7(no5)
Bdim7
A♭/C
C♯dim7
C♯maj7(no5)
D♯madd♯11
D♯7(no5)
A♭sus2
T
A
B

Chromatic Movement Over Minor Scale

study designed by Carlos Brizzola

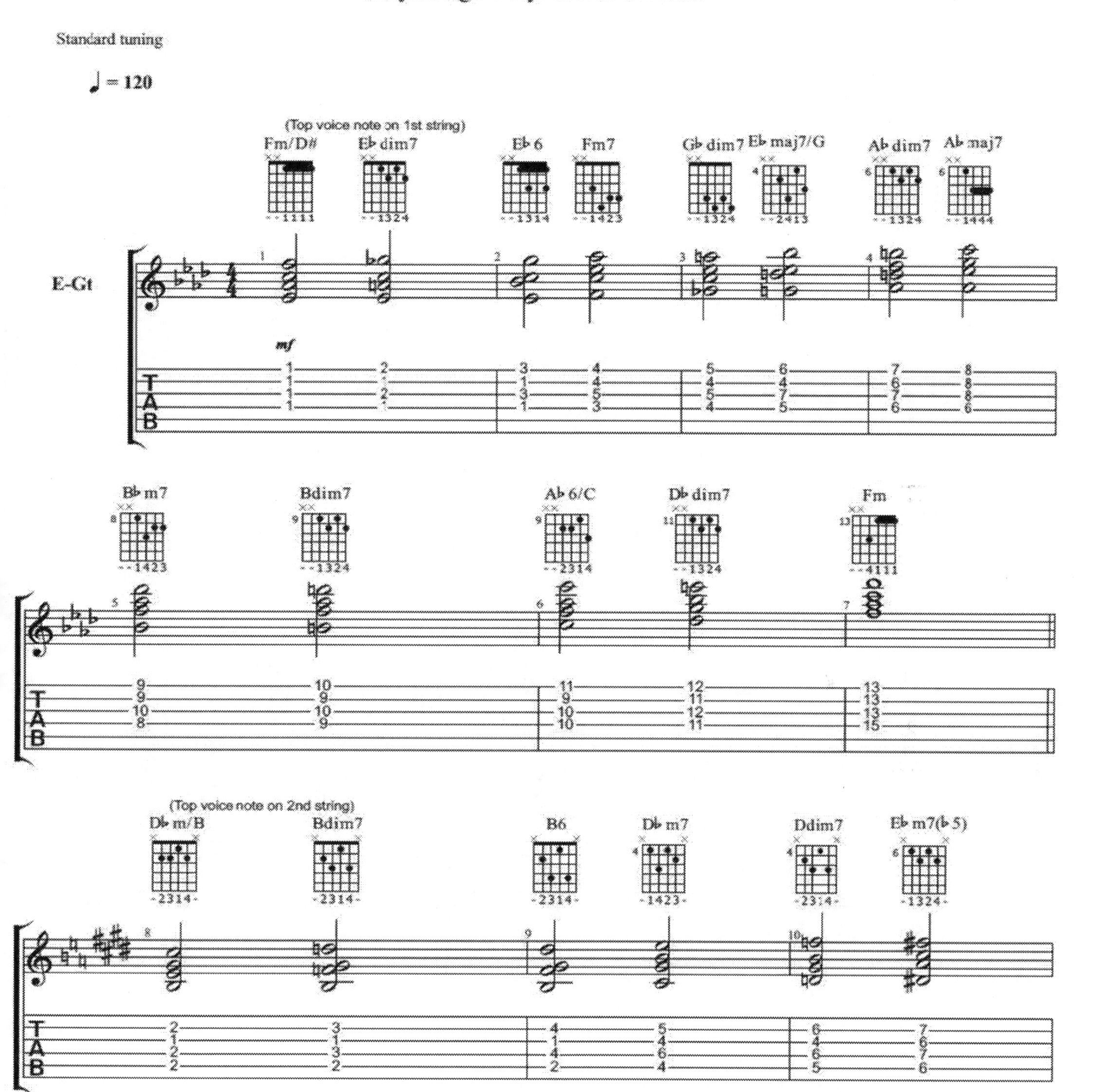

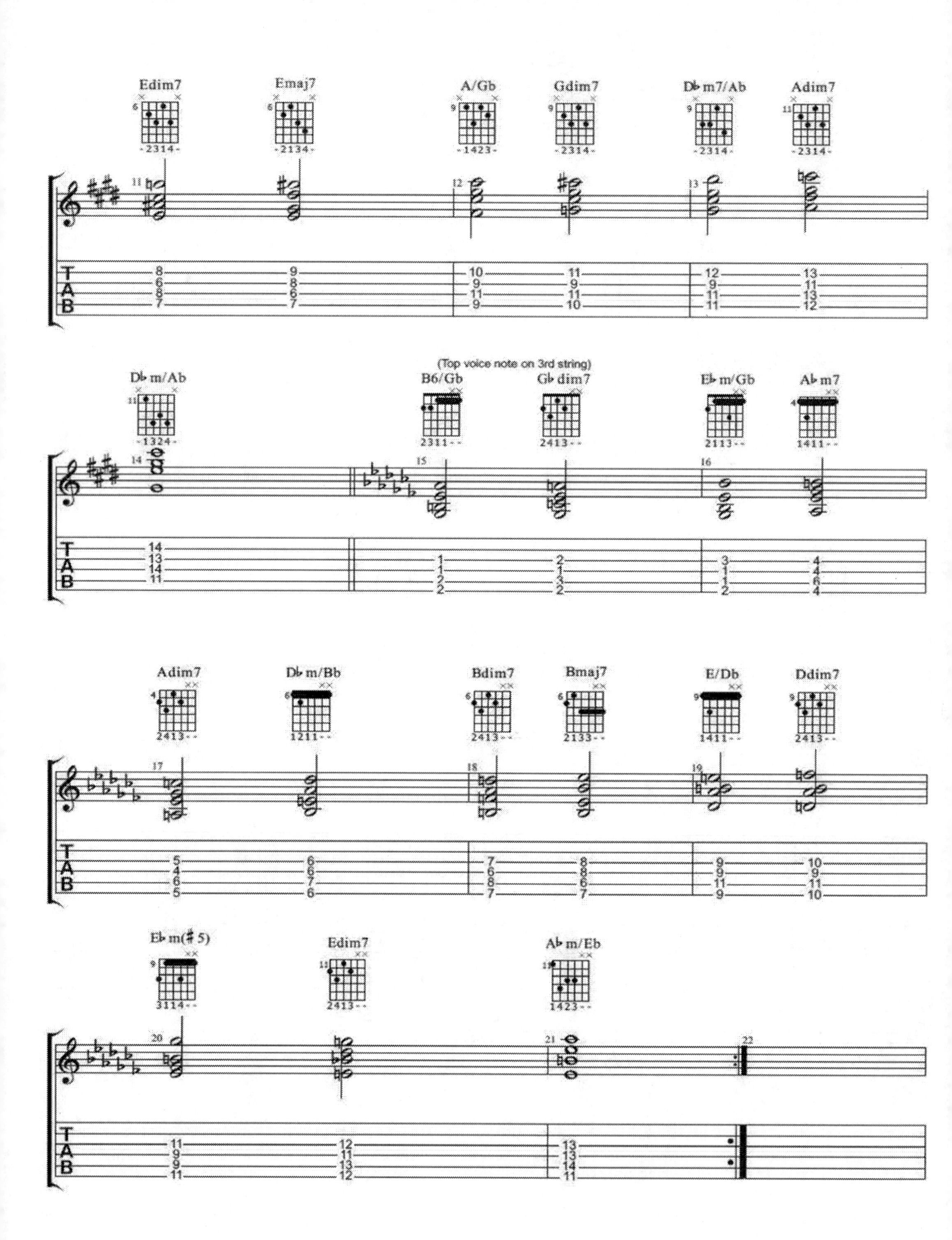
Edim7
Emaj7
A/Gb
Gdim7
D♭m7/Ab
Adim7
D♭m/Ab
(Top voice note on 3rd string)
B6/Gb
G♭dim7
E♭m/Gb
A♭m7
Adim7
D♭m/Bb
Bdim7
Bmaj7
E/Db
Ddim7
E♭m(♯5)
Edim7
A♭m/Eb

Chromatic Movement Over Dominant Scale

study designed by Carlos Brizzola

Standard tuning

♩ = 120

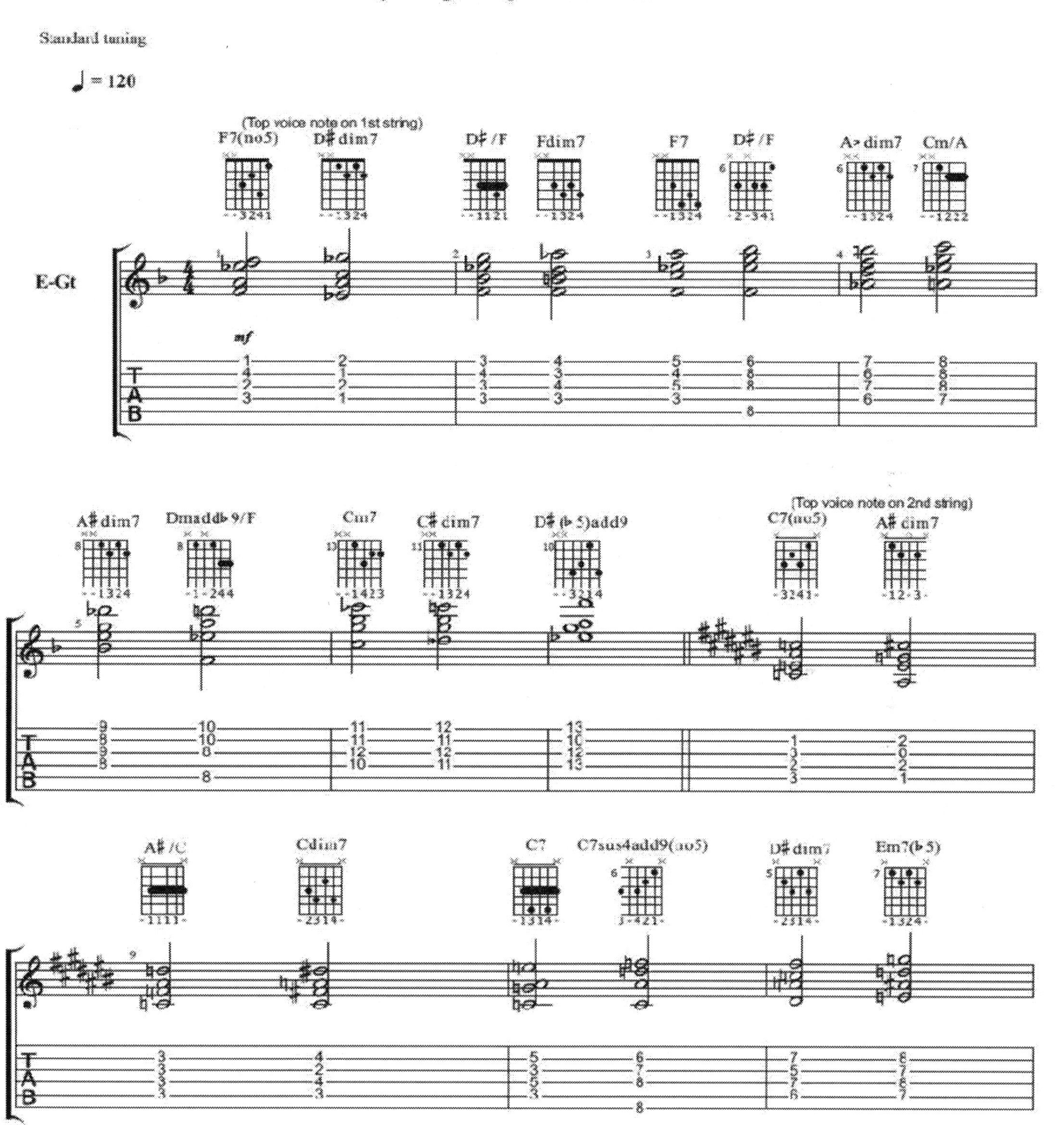

Fdim7
Amadd♭9/C
Gm7
A♭dim7
A♯(♭5)add9
(Top voice note on 3rd string)
G7(no5)
Fdim7
F/G
Gdim7
G7
F/C
A♯dim7
Dm/B
Cdim7
Bsus4(♭5)
Dm7
D♯dim7
Gadd9/D

How To Arrange A Song - Step 1

Stablishing the melody and chord progression

study designed by Carlos Brizzola

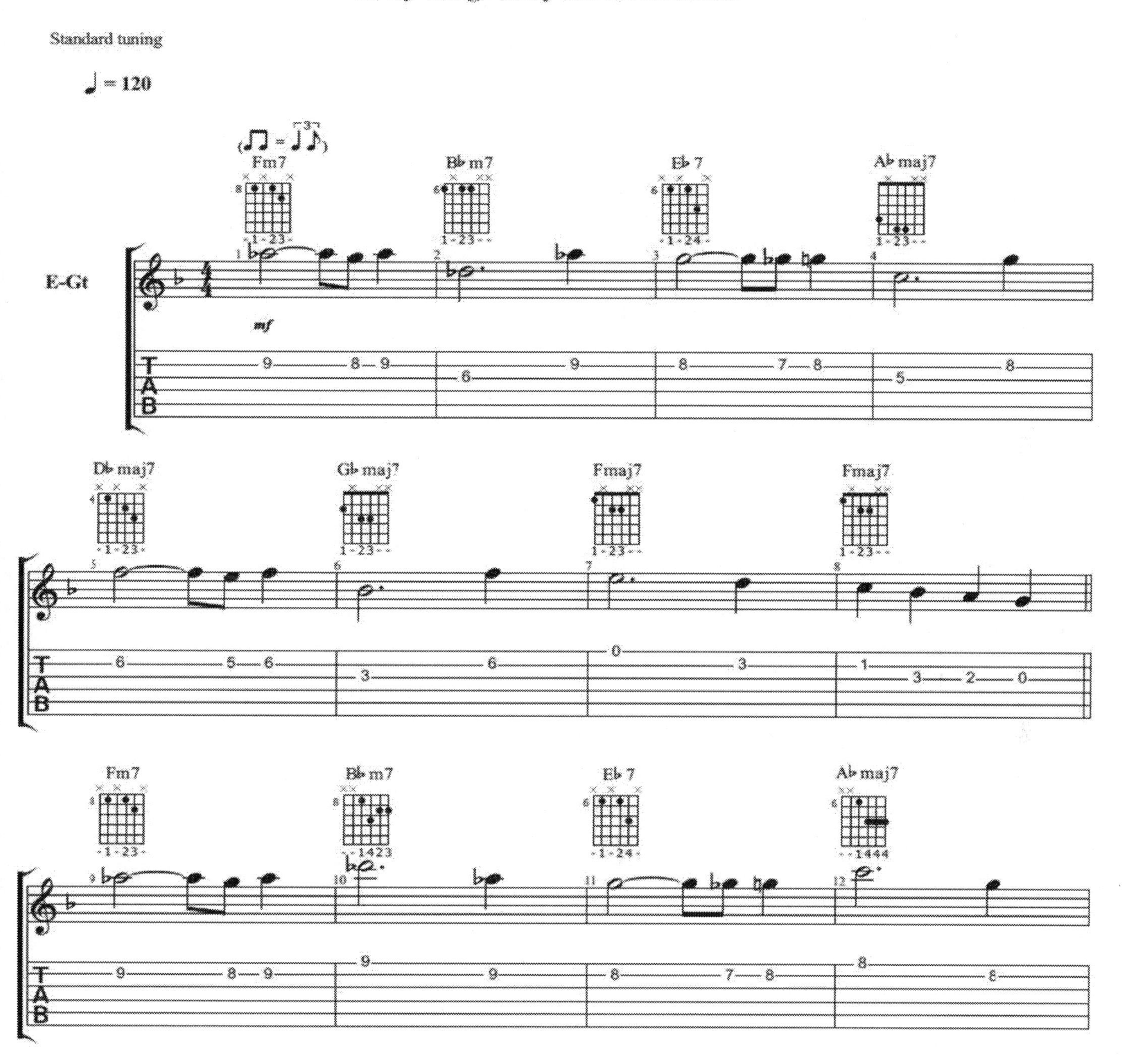

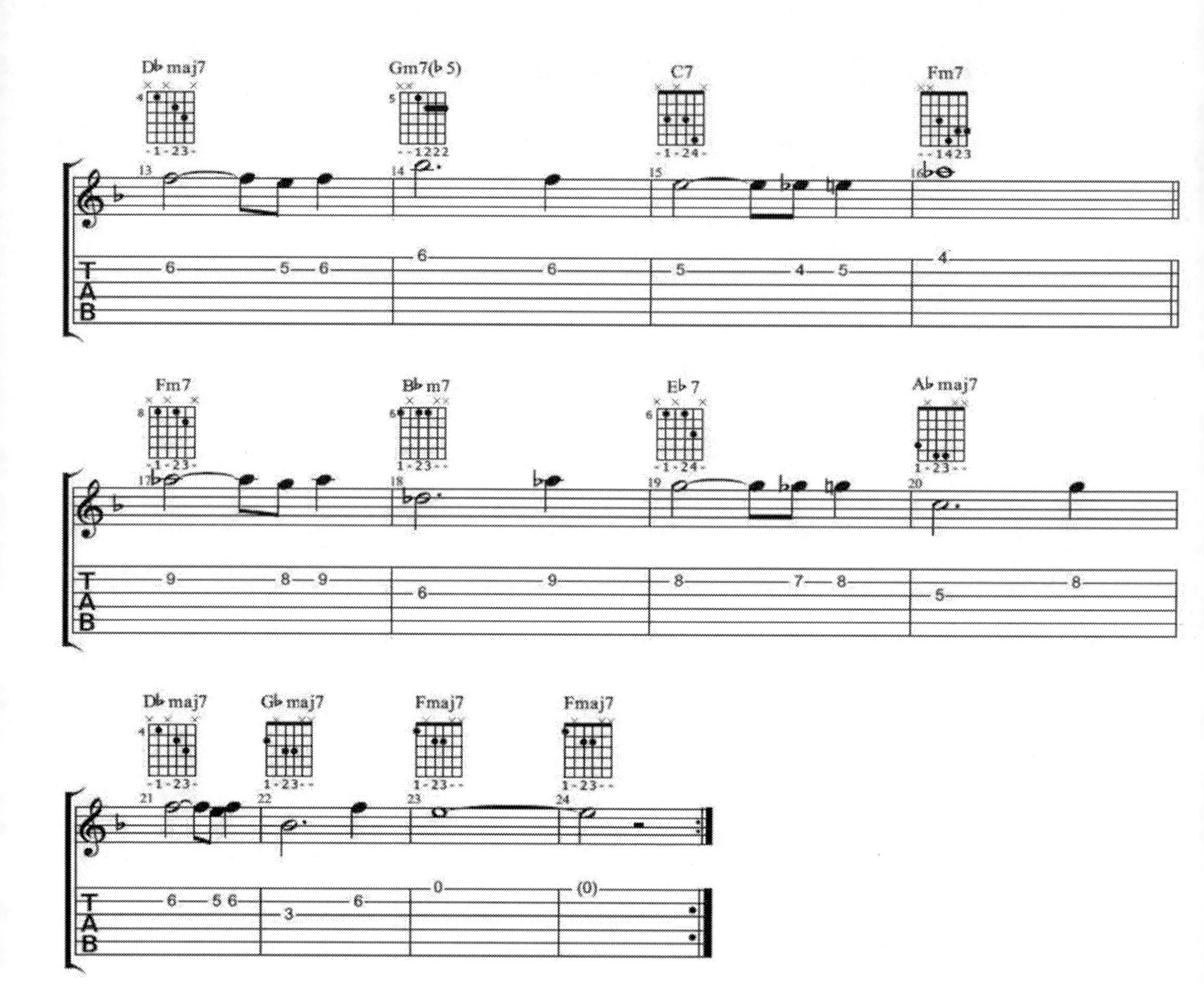

D♭maj7
Gm7(♭5)
C7
Fm7
Fm7
B♭m7
E♭7
A♭maj7
D♭maj7
G♭maj7
Fmaj7
Fmaj7

How To Arrange A Song - Step 2

play the melody with the root note of the chord

Study designed by Carlos Brizzola

Db maj7
Gm7(b5)
C7
Fm7
Fm7
Bb m7
Eb 7
Ab maj7
Db maj7
Gb maj7
Fmaj7
Fmaj7

How To Arrange A Song - Step 3

using chords as part of the melody alternating with single notes

Study designed by Carlos Brizzola

Fmaj7(♭5)
EXAMPLE 2
Fm7
Em7
Fm7
B♭m7
Cm7
D♭maj7
E♭7
D7
E♭7
A♭maj7
B♭m7
Cm7
D♭maj7
Cmaj7
D♭maj7
G♭maj7
Am7
B♭m7

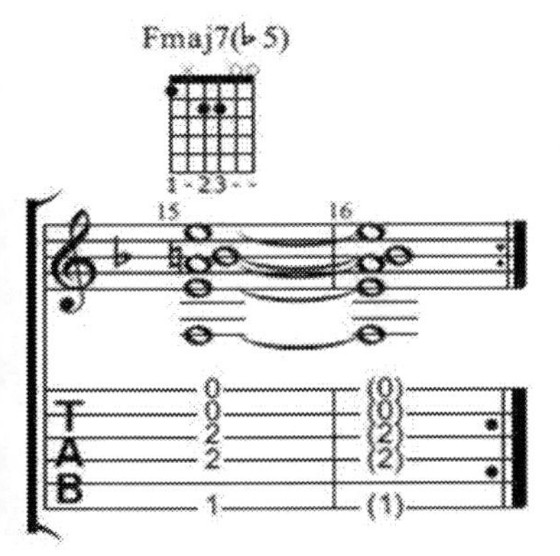
Fmaj7(♭5)
1 - 2 3 - -
15
16
T
A
B
0
0
2
2
1
(0)
(0)
(2)
(2)
(1)

Study #1

alternating chords and notes

study over II-V-I designed by Carlos Brizzola

Standard tuning

♩ = 120

II V I I - in Ab major II V I I - in F major

Bb m7 A7 Ab maj7 Ab 6 Gm7 Gb 7 Fmaj7 Dm7/F

E-Gt

mf

II V I I - in Eb major II V I I - in C major

Fm7 E7 Eb maj7 Eb 6 Dm7 Db 7 Cmaj7 C6

II V I I - in Bb major I V I I - in G major

Cm7 B7 Bb maj7 Bb 6 Am7 Ab 7 Gmaj7 G6

Study #2

alternating chords and notes

study over II-V-I designed by Carlos Brizzola

Standard tuning

♩ = 120

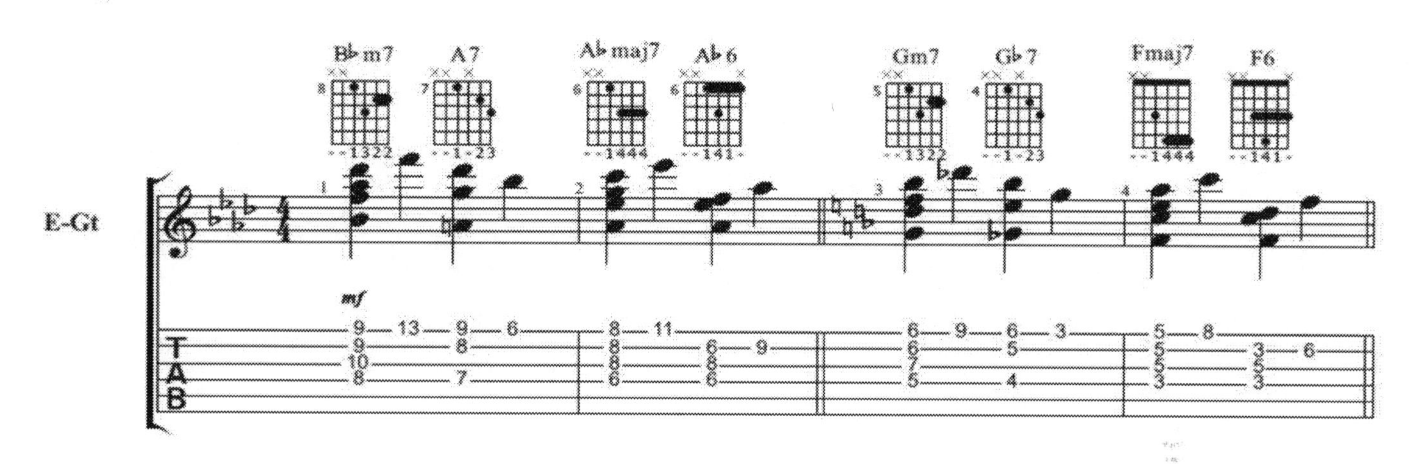

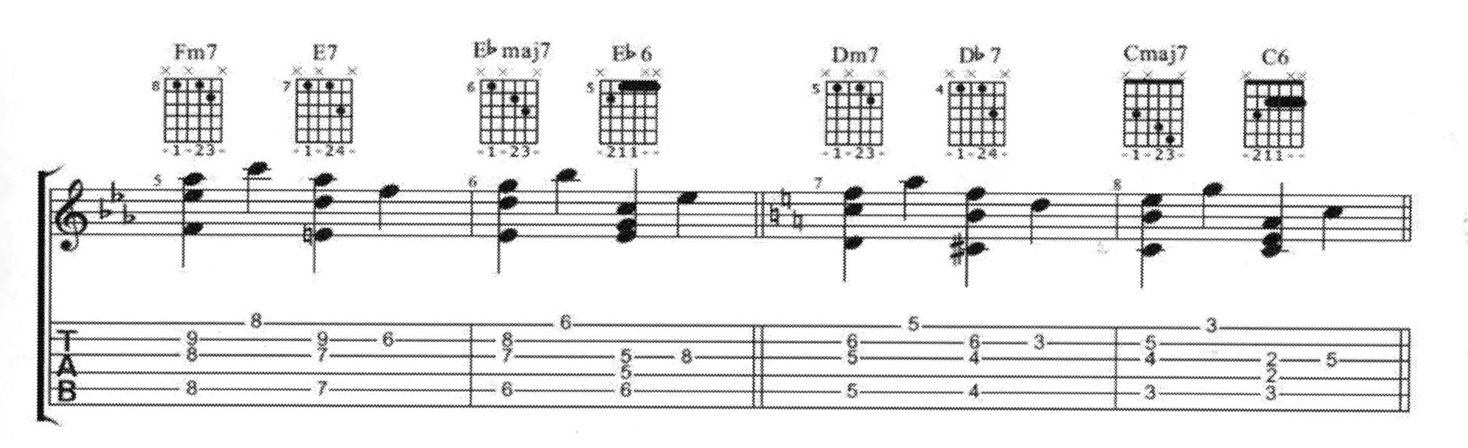

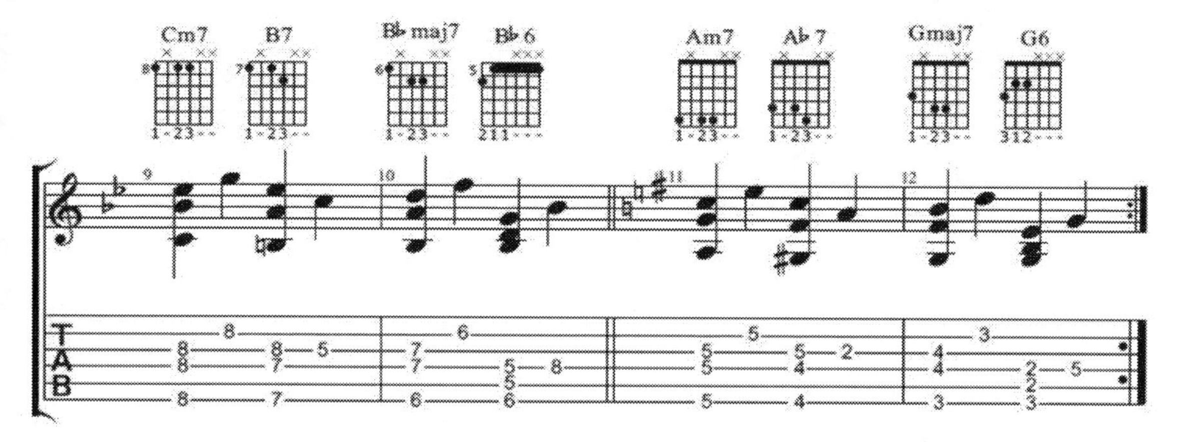

Study #3

alternating chords and notes

study over II-V-I designed by Carlos Brizzola

adding two notes after each chord

Standard tuning

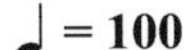 **= 100**

Study #4

alternating chords and notes

study over II-V-I designed by Carlos Brizzola

adding three notes after each chord

Study #5

study over II-V-I designed by Carlos Brizzola

creating melody phrases with chords

matching the chord's top voice note with the melody

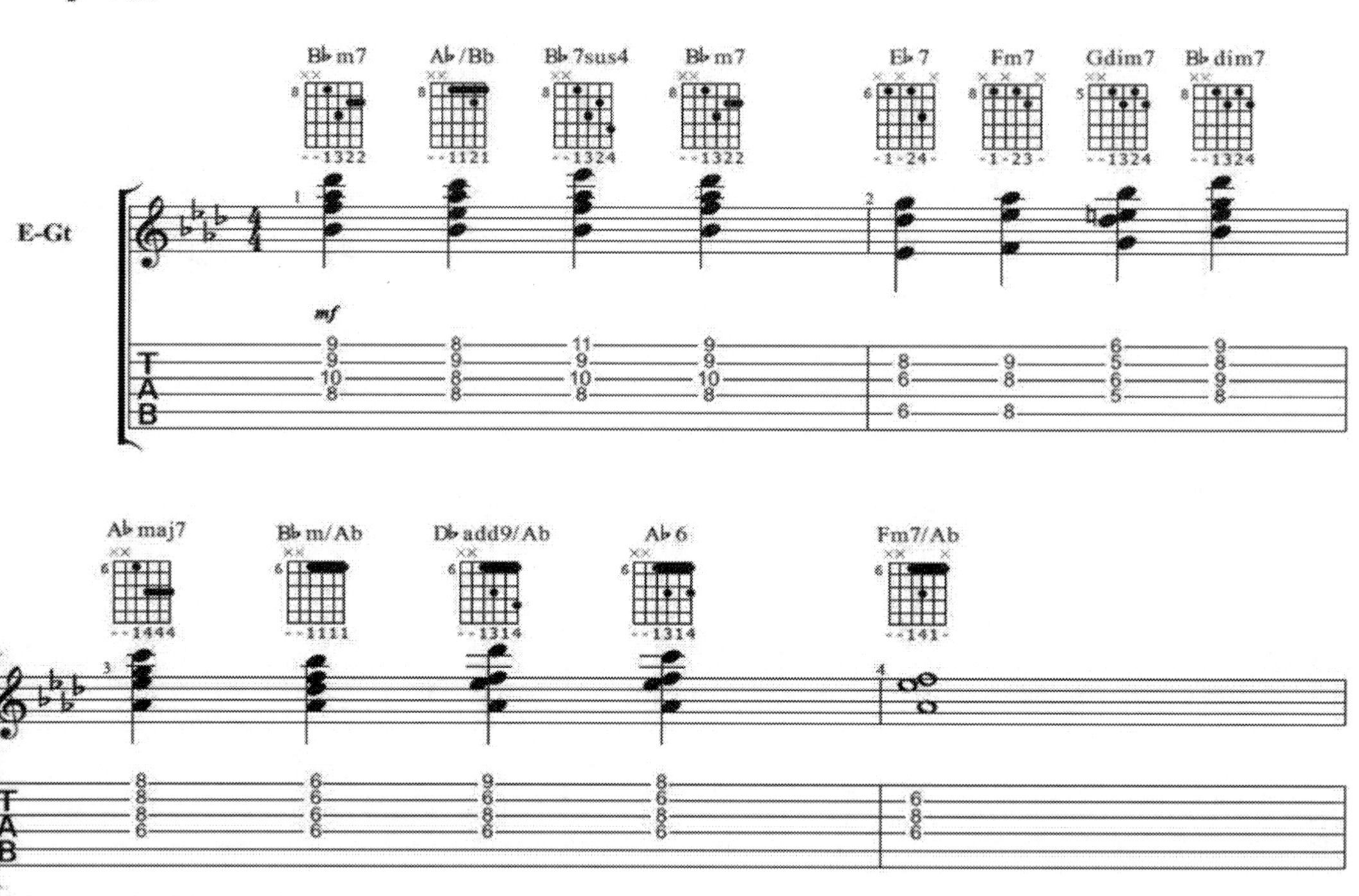

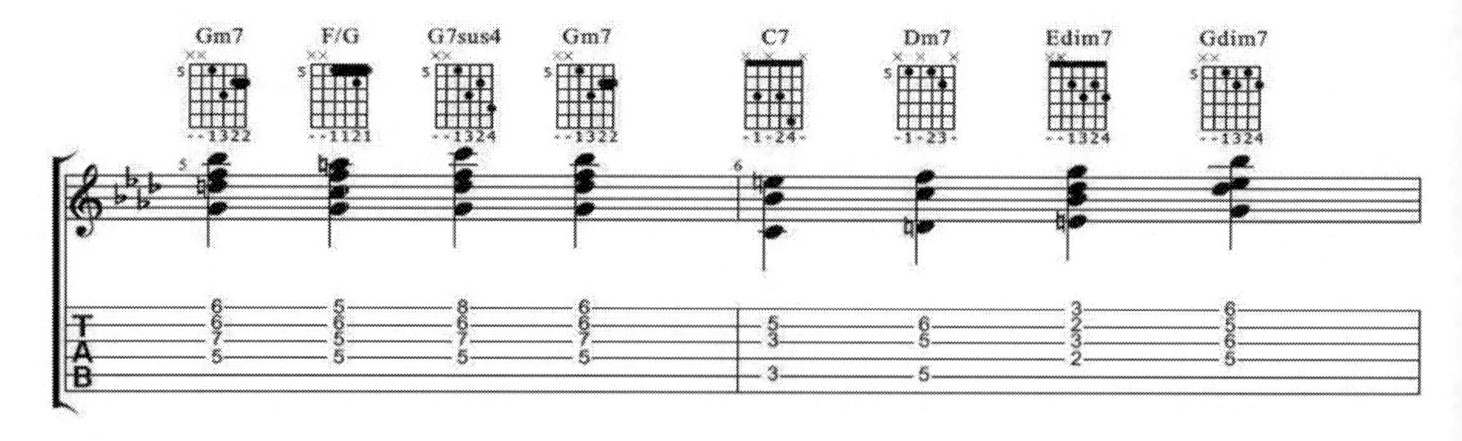

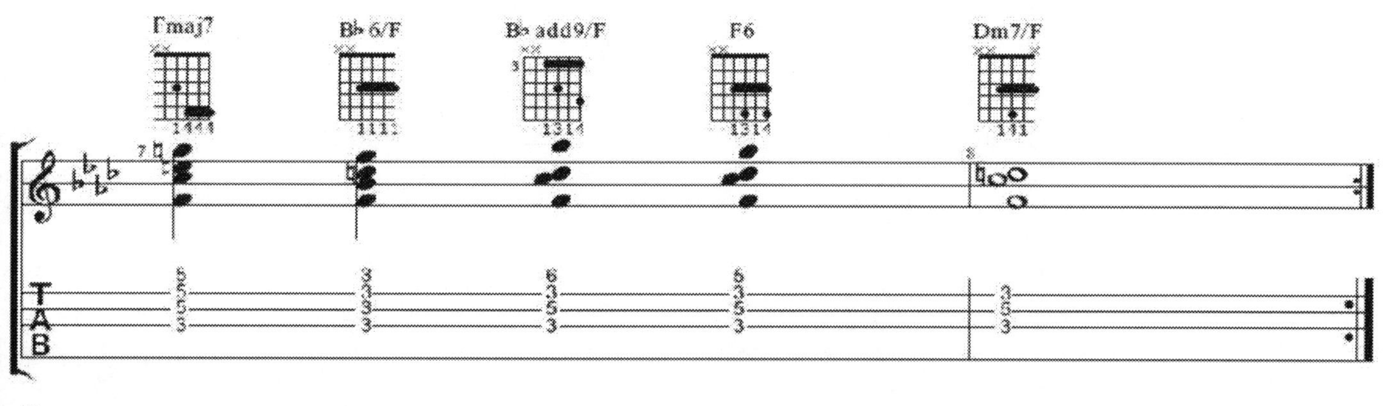
Fmaj7
B♭6/F
B♭add9/F
F6
Dm7/F

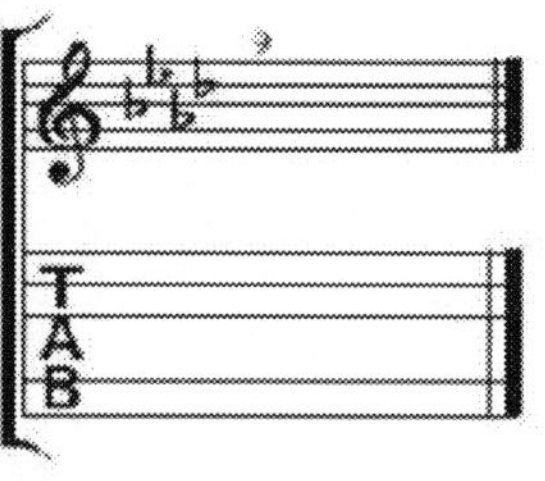

Study #6

study over II-V-I designed by Carlos Brizzola

matching the top voice note of the chord with the melody

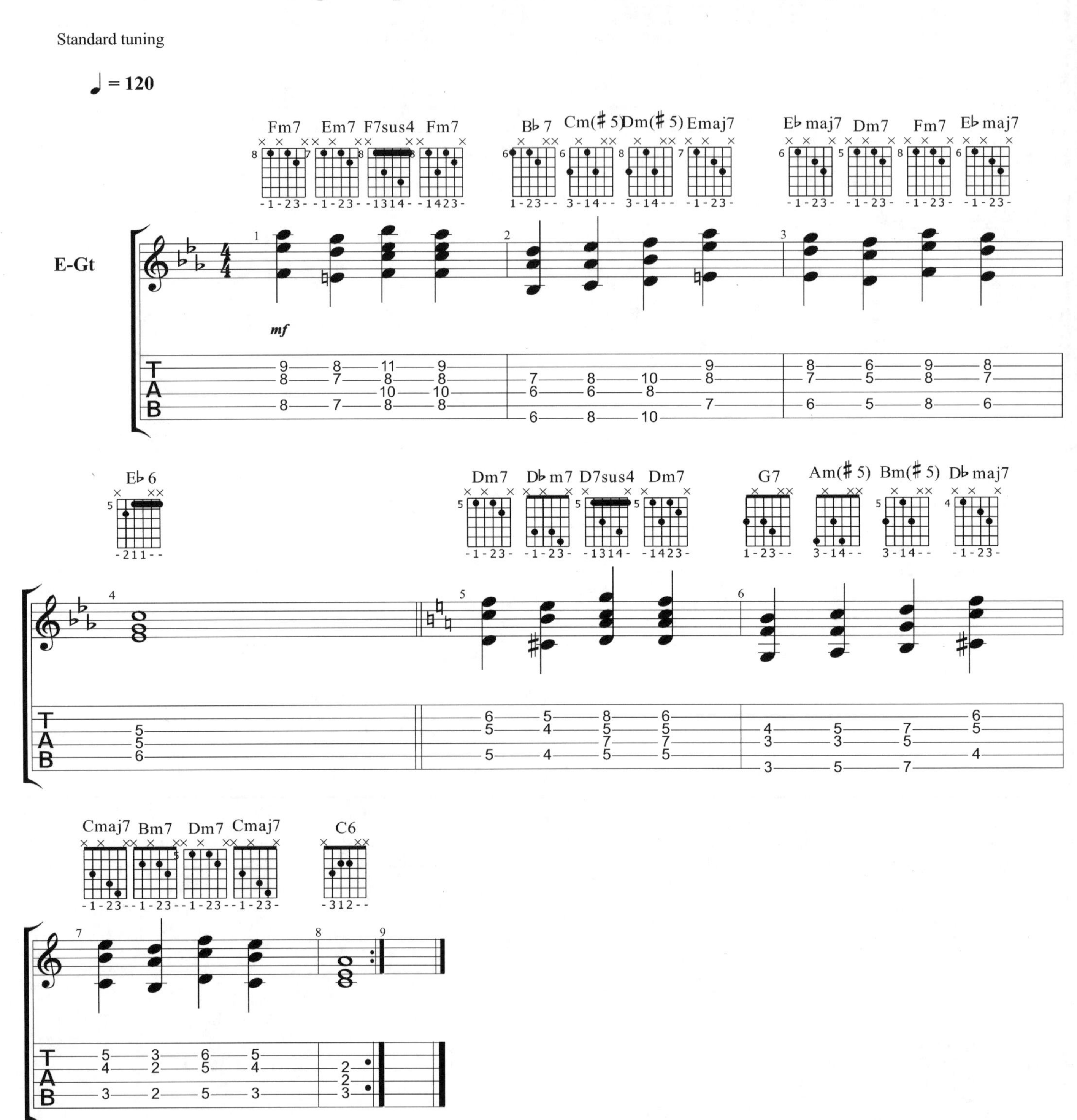

Study #7

study over II-V-I designed by Carlos Brizzola

creating melody phrases with chords

matching the chord's top voice note with the melody

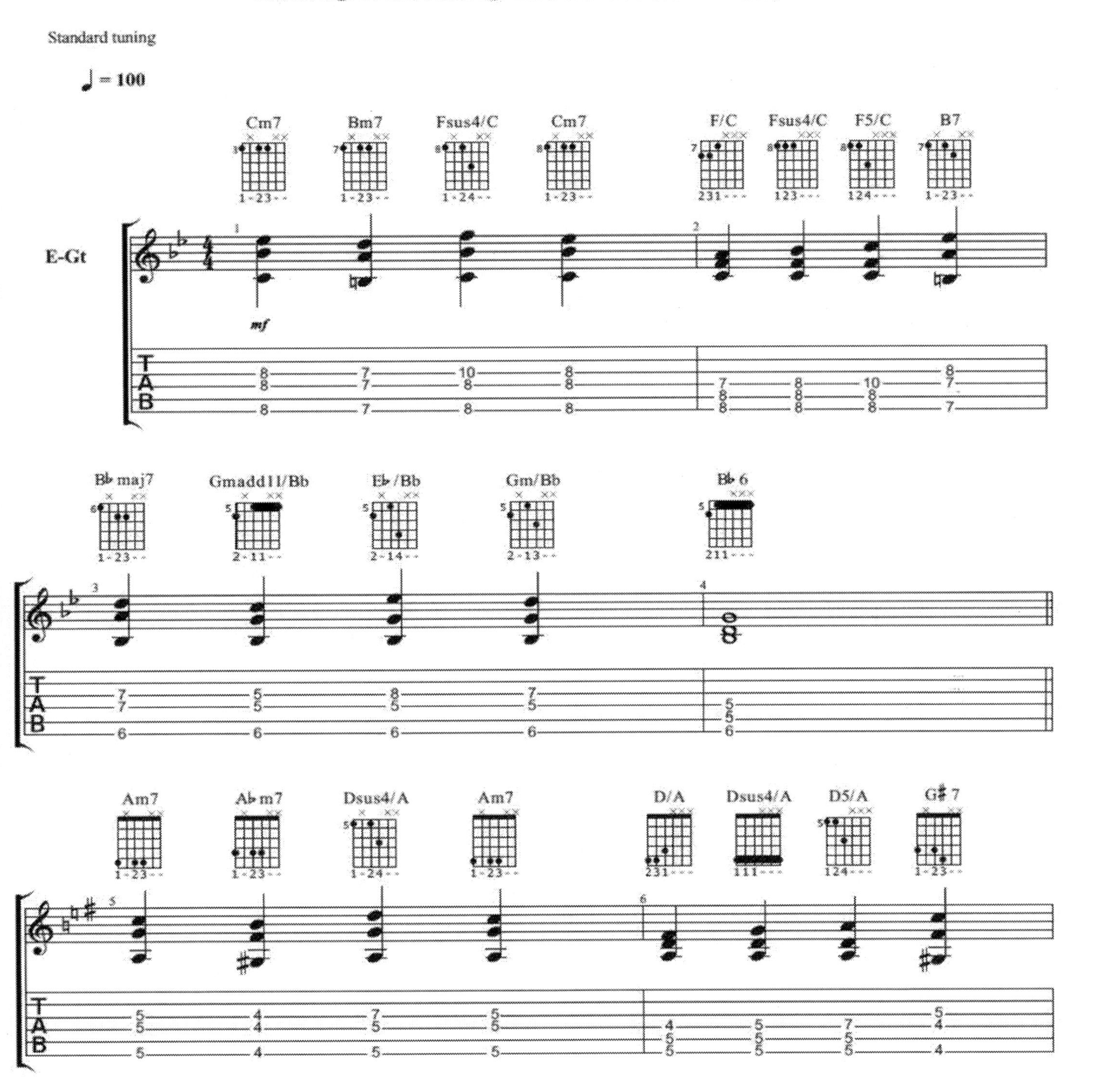

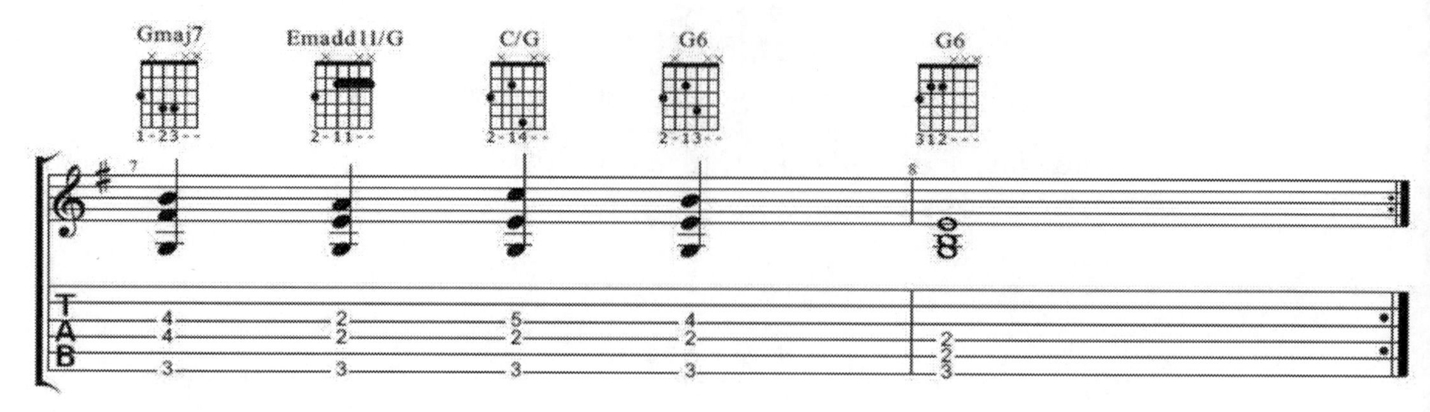
Gmaj7
Emadd11/G
C/G
G6
G6
1 - 2 3 - -
2 - 1 1 - -
2 - 1 4 - -
2 - 1 3 - -
3 1 2 - - -
7
8
T
A
B
4
4
3
2
2
3
5
2
3
4
2
3
2
2
3

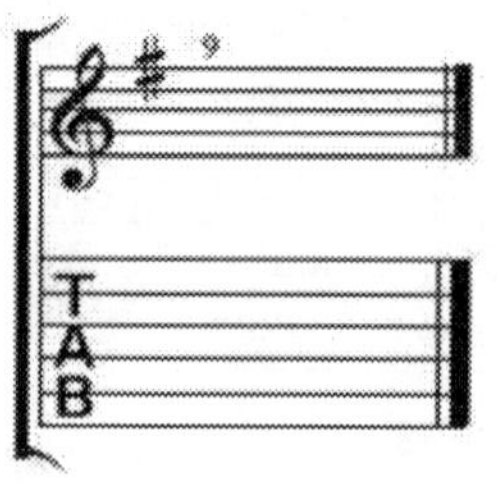
9
T
A
B

Study #8

study over II-V-I designed by Carlos Brizzola

creating melody phrases with chords

matching the chord's top voice note with the melody

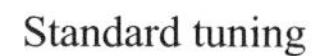

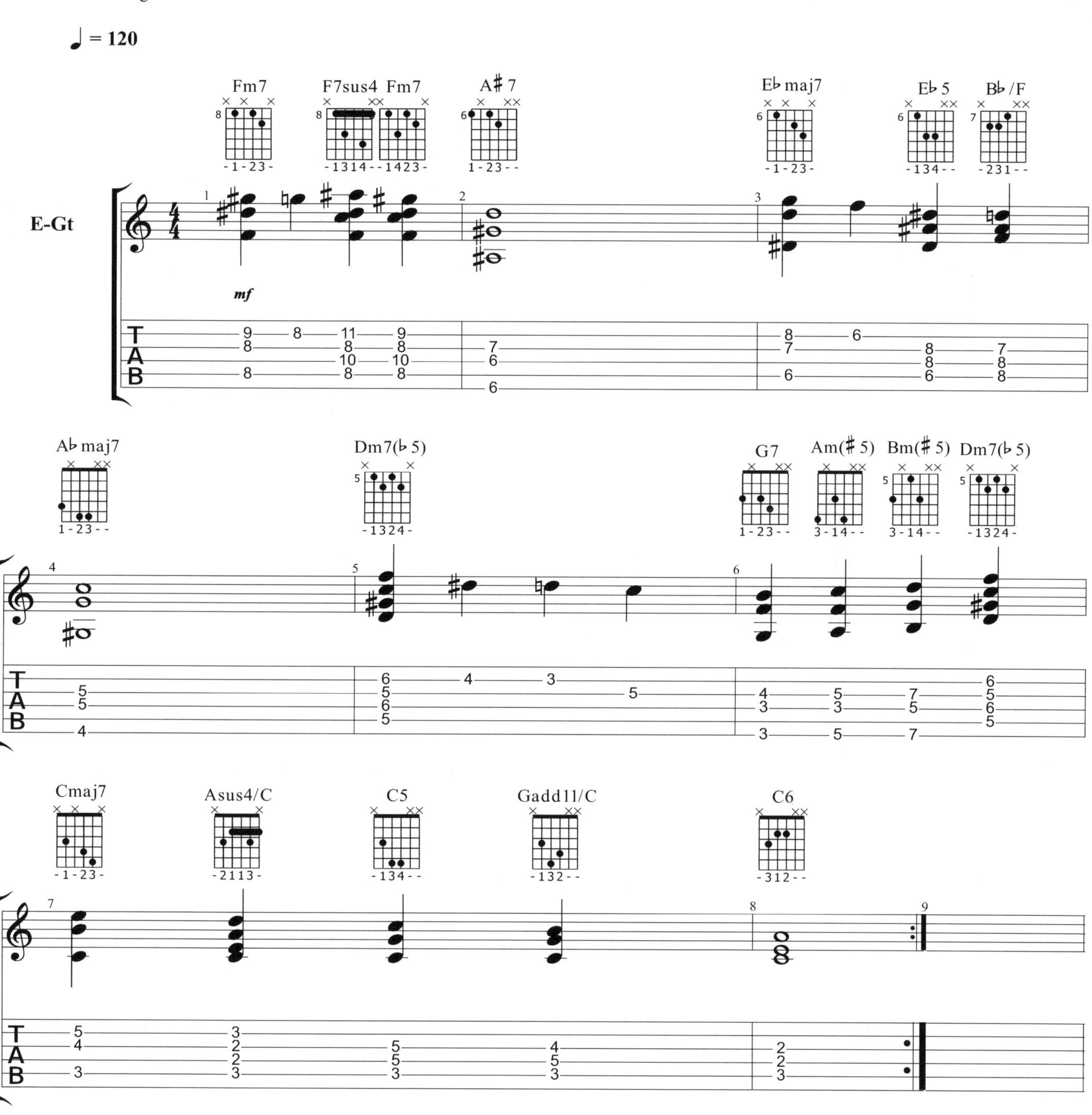

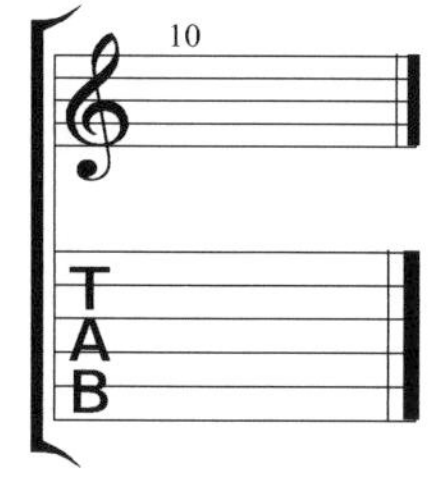

Study #9

study over II-V-I designed by Carlos Brizzola
creating melody phrases with chords
matching the chord's top voice note with the melody

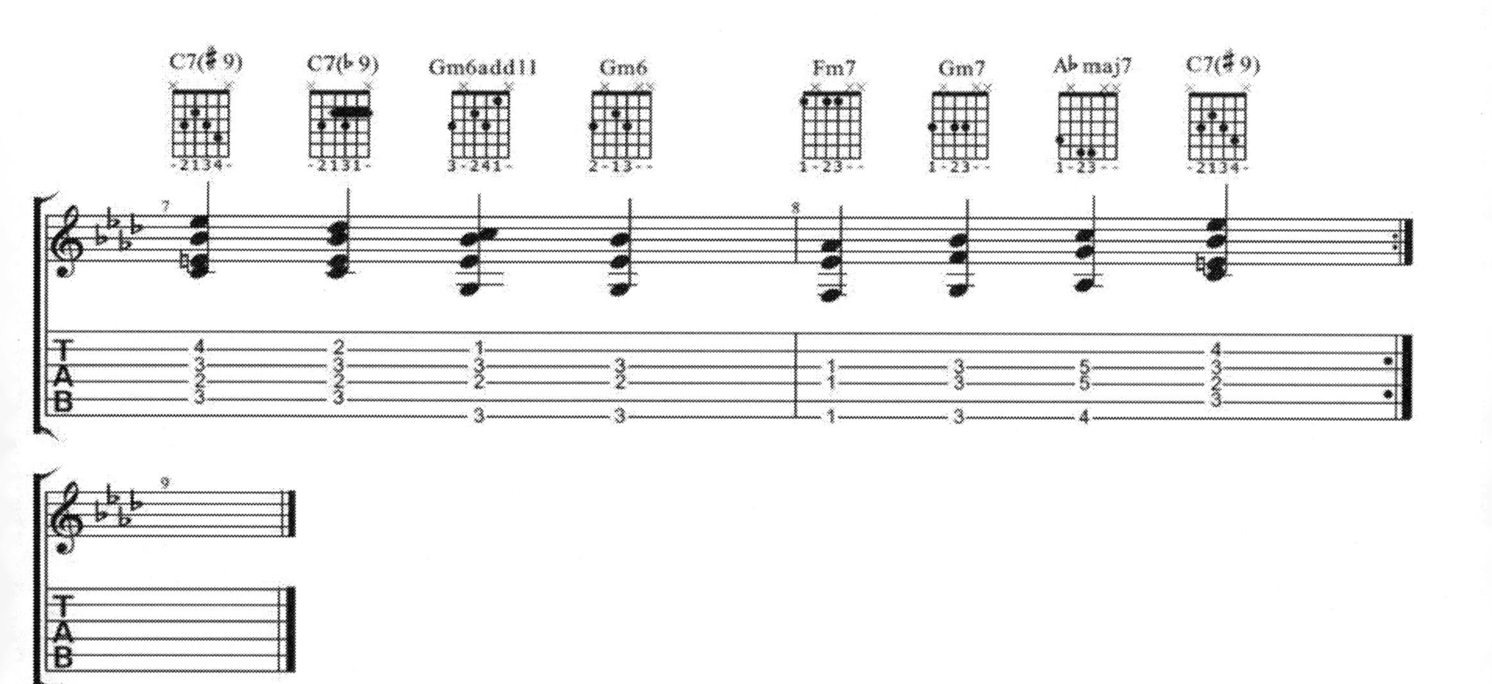
C7(♯9)
C7(♭9)
Gm6add11
Gm6
Fm7
Gm7
A♭maj7
C7(♯9)

Study #10 - Creating melody phrases with chords

study over ii-V-I designed by Carlos Brizzola

matching the top voice note of the chord with the melody

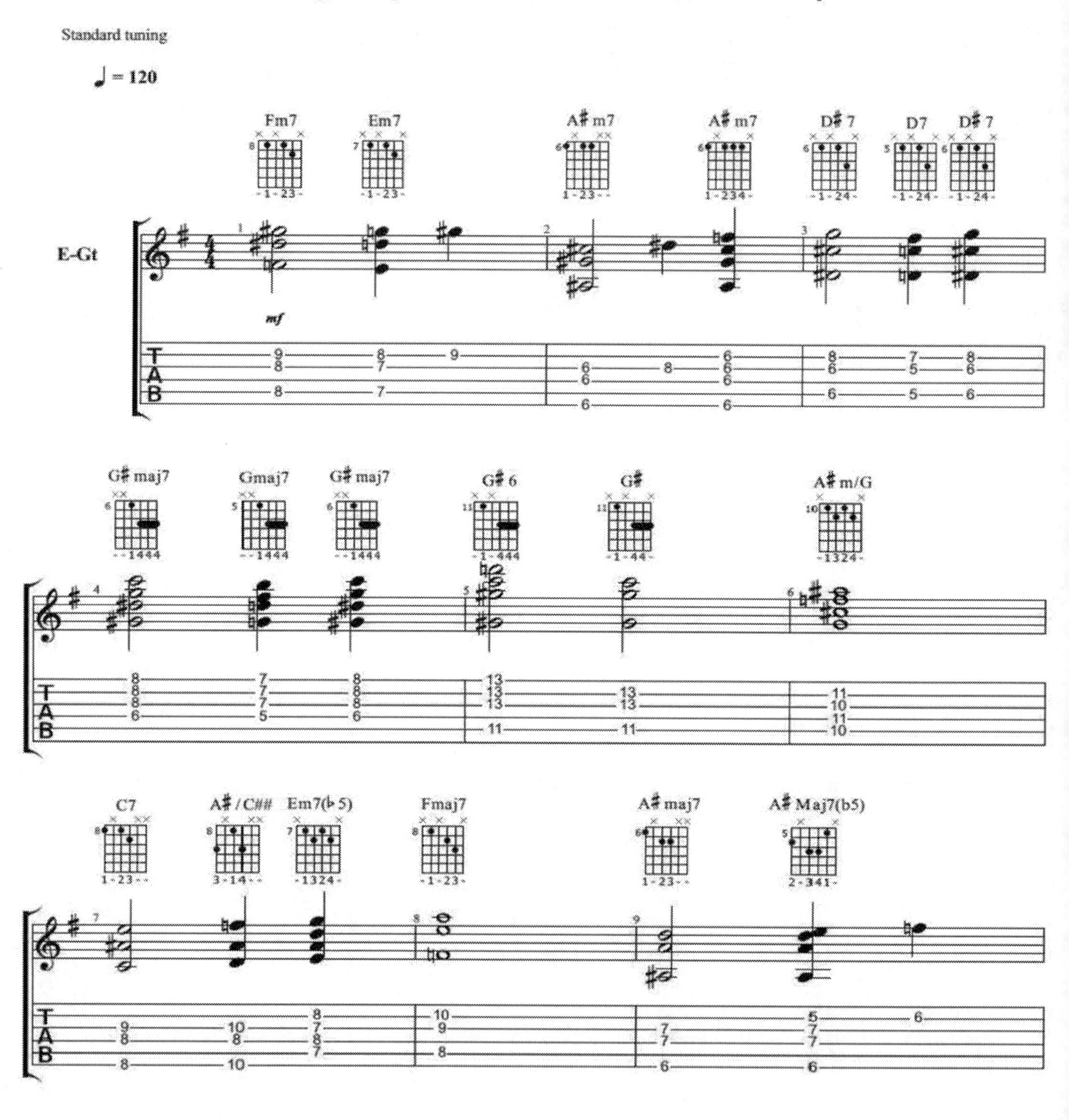

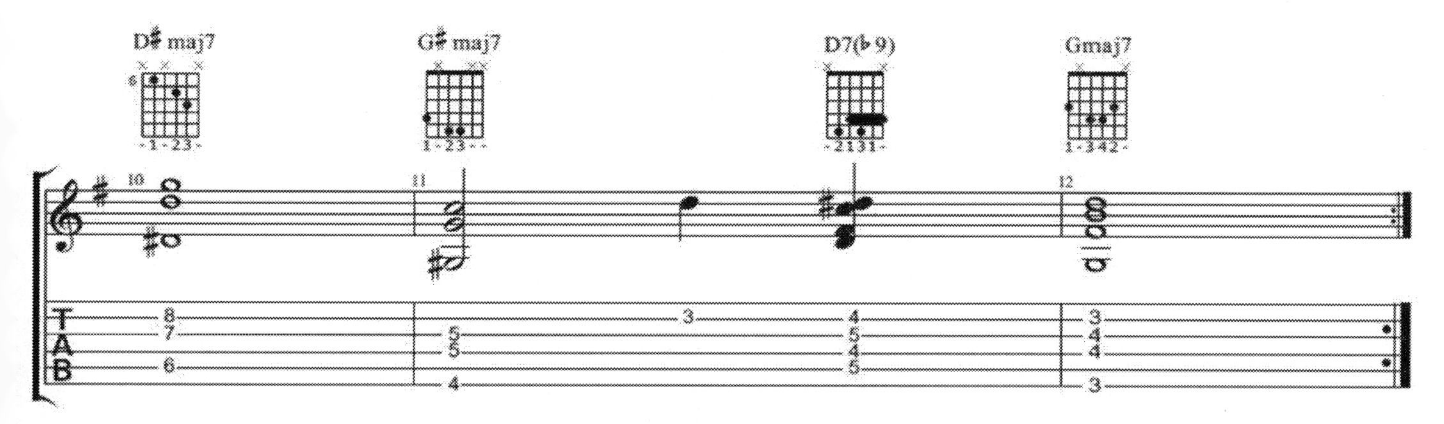
D♯ maj7
G♯ maj7
D7(♭9)
Gmaj7
T
A
B

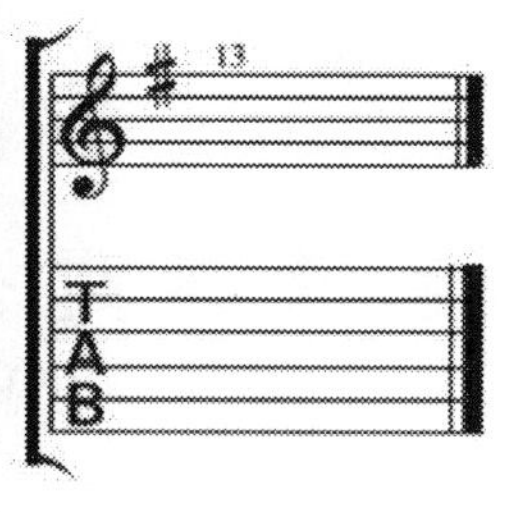
T
A
B

Study #11

created over "All the Things You Are" chord progression.

study designed by Carlos Brizzola

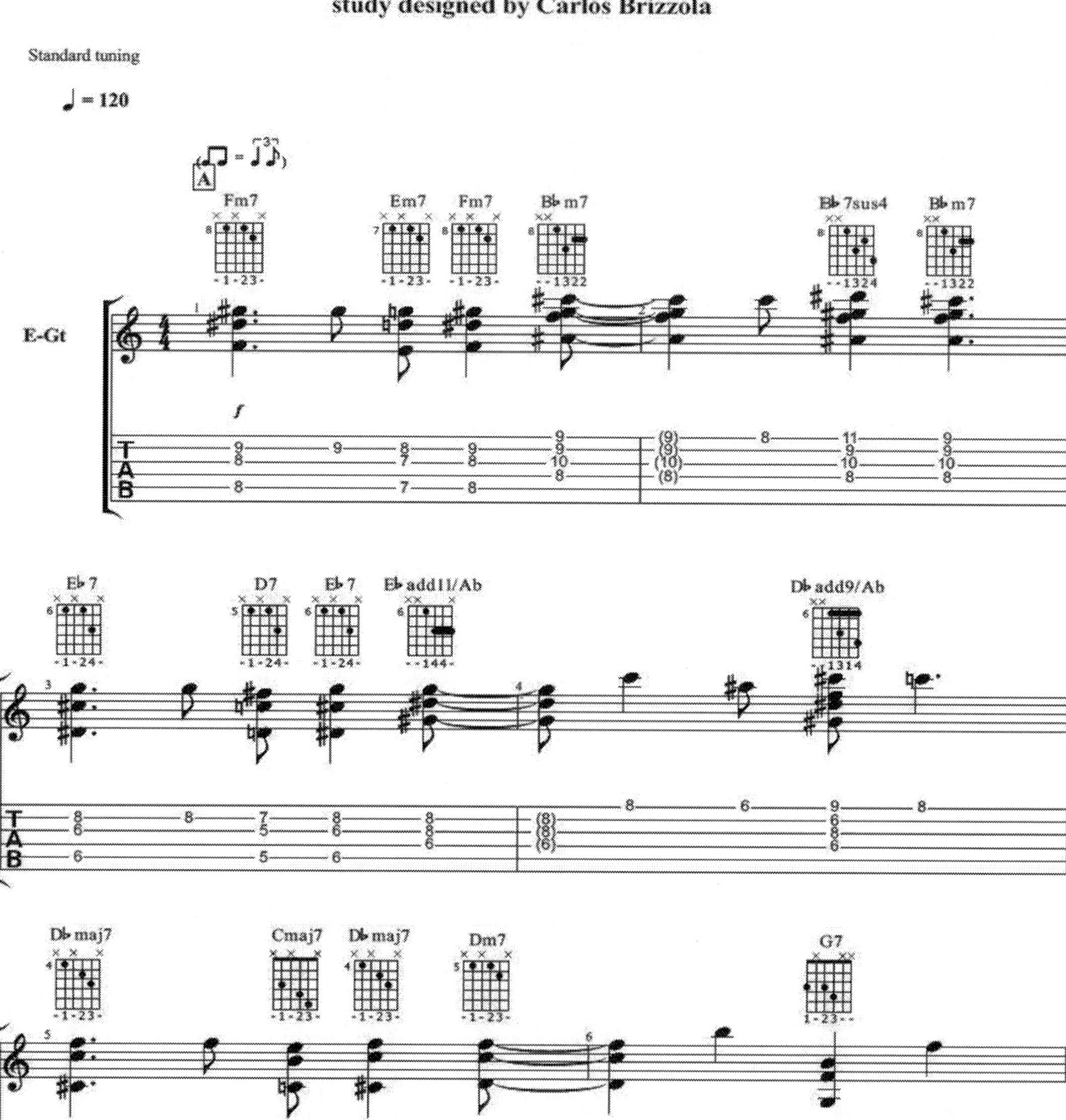

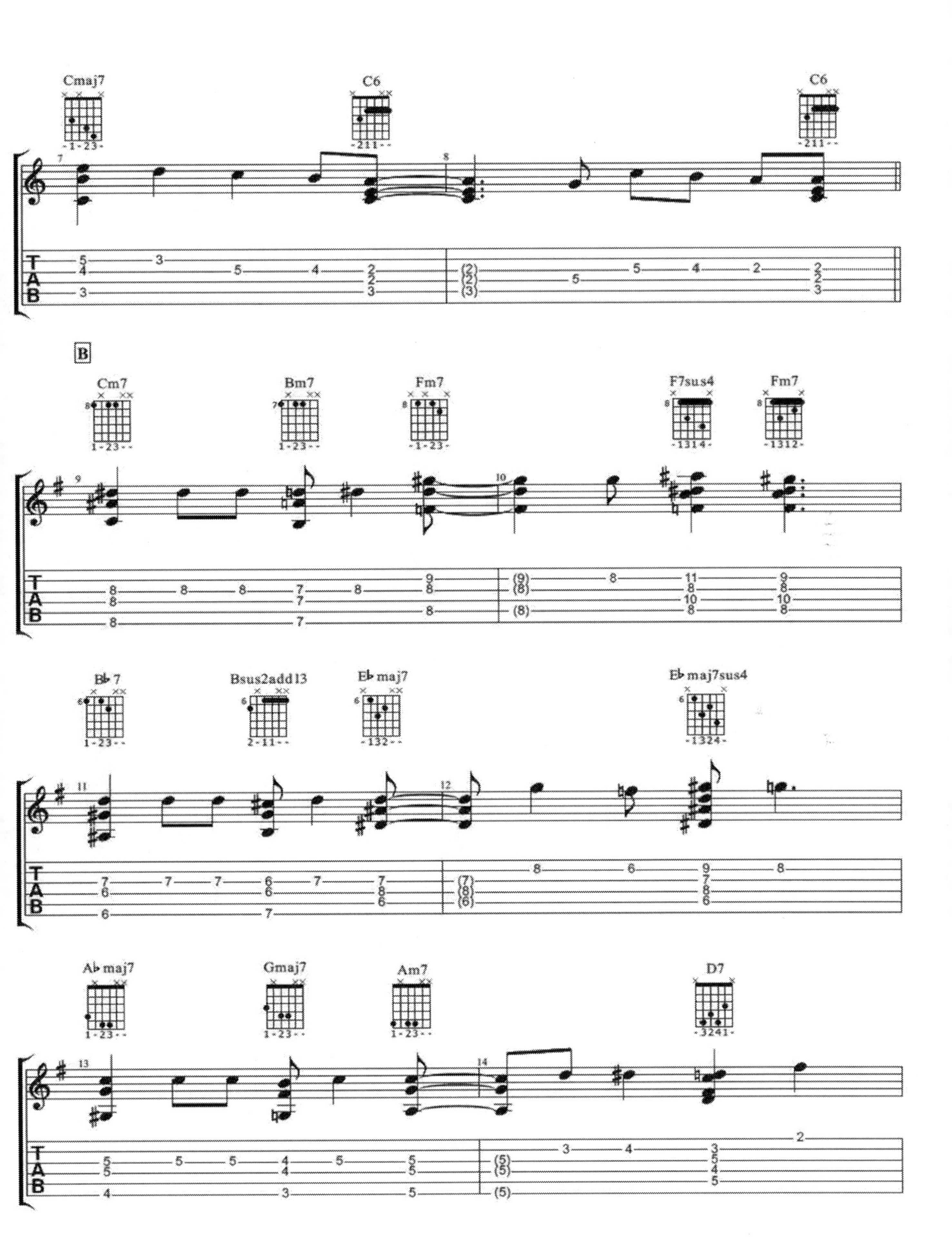
Cmaj7
C6
C6
B
Cm7
Bm7
Fm7
F7sus4
Fm7
B♭7
Bsus2add13
E♭maj7
E♭maj7sus4
A♭maj7
Gmaj7
Am7
D7

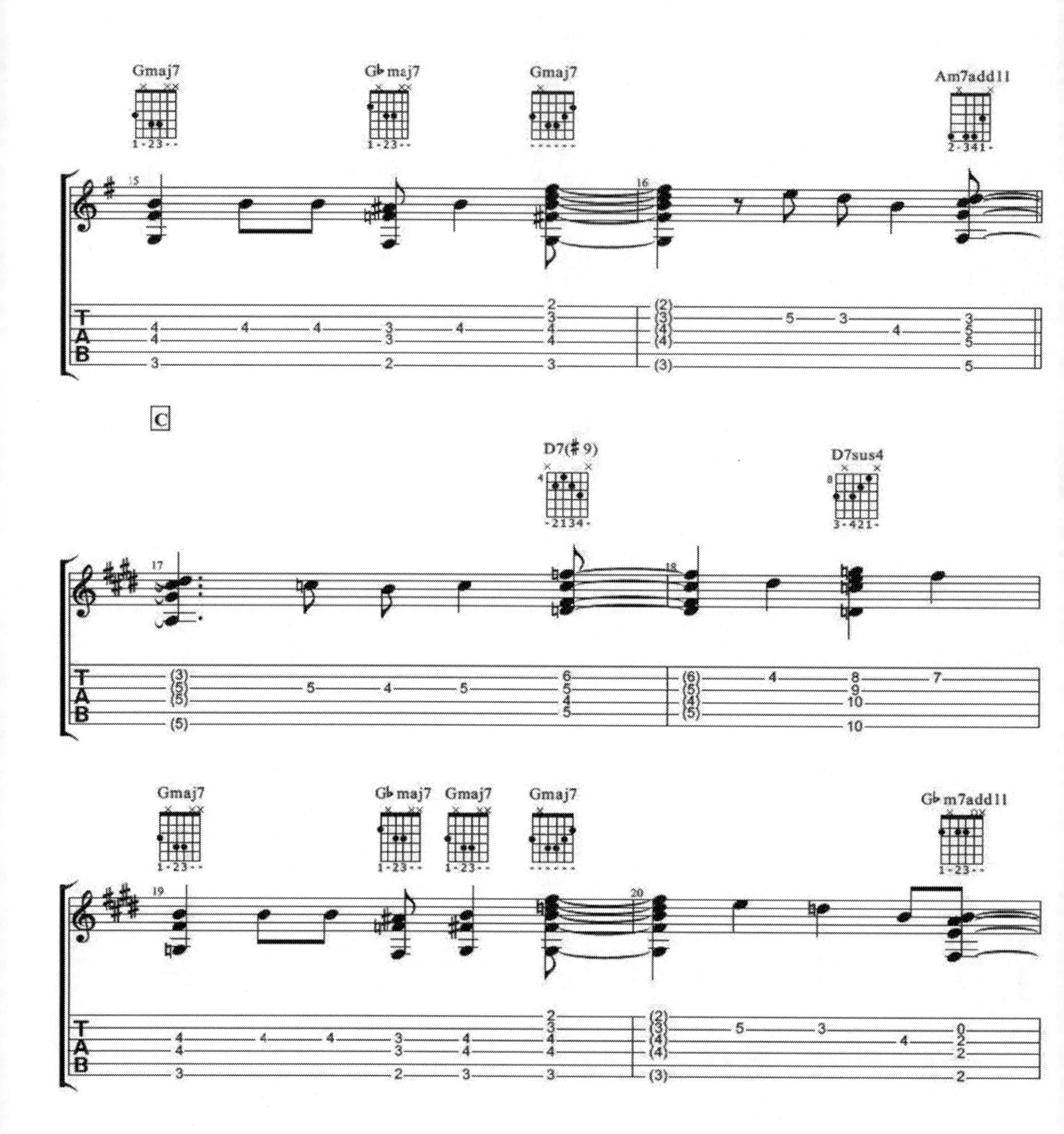
Gmaj7
G♭maj7
Gmaj7
Am7add11
C
D7(♯9)
D7sus4
Gmaj7
G♭maj7
Gmaj7
Gmaj7
G♭m7add11

B7(♯9)
B7sus4
Emaj7
E♭maj7
Emaj7
Emaj7add13
D
Fm7
Em7
Fm7
B♭m7
B♭7sus4
B♭m7
E♭7
D7
E♭7
E♭add11/A♭
A♭sus4add13

D♭maj7
Cmaj7
D♭maj7
B♭sus4(♭5)
Cm7
Bm7
Cm7
Bm6(♯5)
B♭m7
B♭m7
D♭6
G
A♭
A♭maj7(♭5)
T
A
B

Study #12

created over"The Shadow Of Your Smile" chord progression

study designed by Carlos Brizzola

Standard tuning

♩ = 120

F♯m7
B7
B7
Em7
Em7/D
C♯m7(♭5)
C7
B7
C7
B7
2.
Bm7(♭5)
G♯6(♭5)
G♯dim7
Am7add11
Cm7add11
Bm7add11

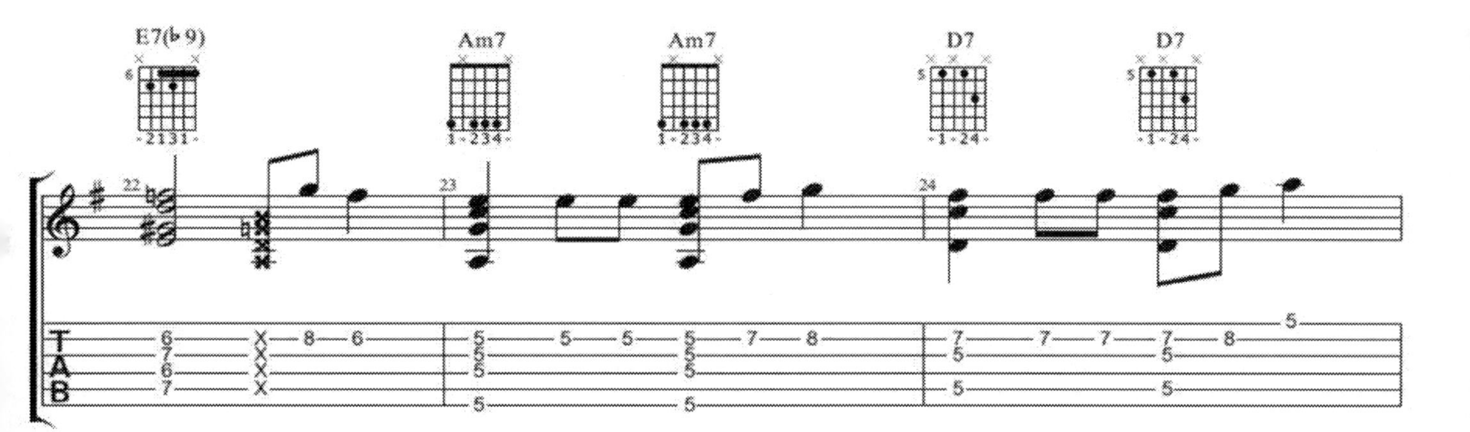
E7(♭9)
Am7
Am7
D7
D7

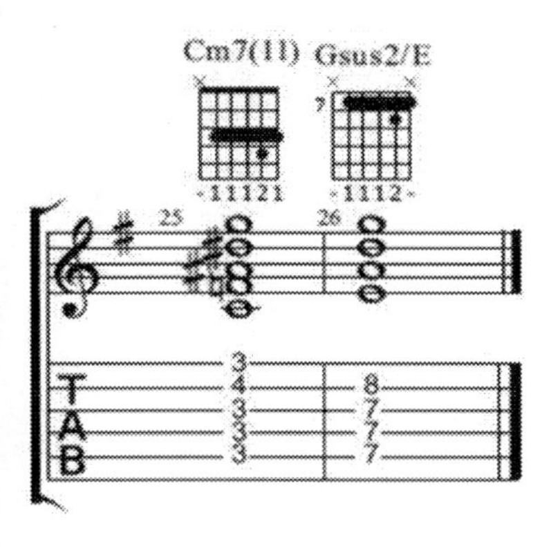
Cm7(11)
Gsus2/E

Study #13

created over "Fly Me To The Moon" chord progression

study designed by Carlos Brizzola

C7(#9)
C7(b9)
Fm7
Fm7
B
Fm7
Gm7
Adim7
Cdim7
Bb m7
Bb 7sus4
Bb m7
Eb 7
Fm7
Gdim7
Bb dim7
Ab maj7
Db add9/Ab
Ab 6
Db maj7
Em7
Fm7
Adim7
Gm7(b5)
G7sus4
Gm7
C7

Dm7
Edim7
Gdim7
Fm7
F7sus4
Fm7
Am7
C
B♭m7
B♭m7
E♭7
E♭7sus4
Cm7
F7(♯9)
F7(♭9)
F7
Am7
B♭m7
B♭m7
E♭9

A♭maj7sus4
A♭maj7
B♭m7
E♭7
D
Fm7
Gm7
Adim7
Cdim7
B♭m7
B♭7sus4
B♭m7
E♭7
Fm7
Gdim7
B♭dim7
A♭maj7
D♭add9/Ab
A♭6
D♭maj7
Em7
Fm7
Adim7
Gm7(♭5)
G7sus4
Gm7
C7

Dm7
Edim7
Gdim7
Fm7
F7sus4
Fm7
Am7
B♭m7
B♭m7
E♭7
E♭7sus4add9
Cm7add11
F7(♯9)
F7(♭9)
Adim7
B♭m11
A♭sus4/Bb
E♭7
E♭7

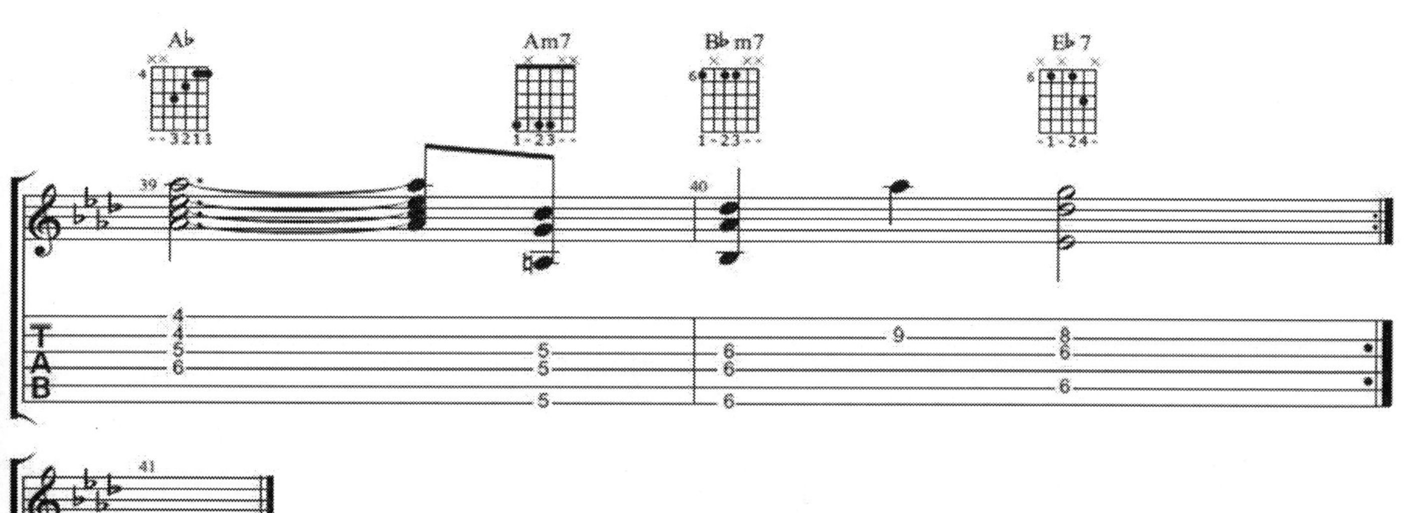
Ab
Am7
Bb m7
Eb 7
39
40
T
A
B

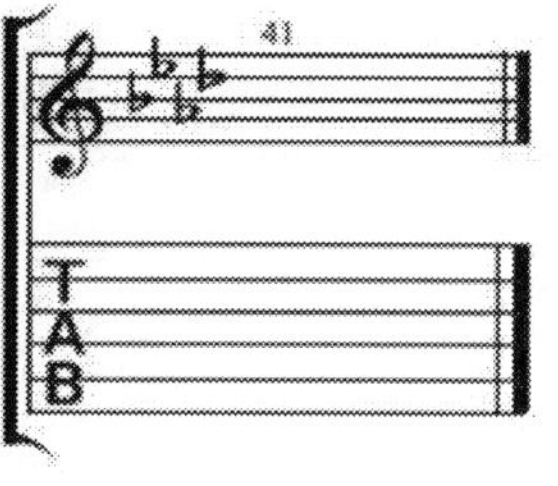
41
T
A
B

Study #14

created over Autumn Leaves chord progression

study designed by Carlos Brizzola

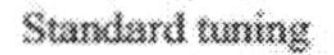

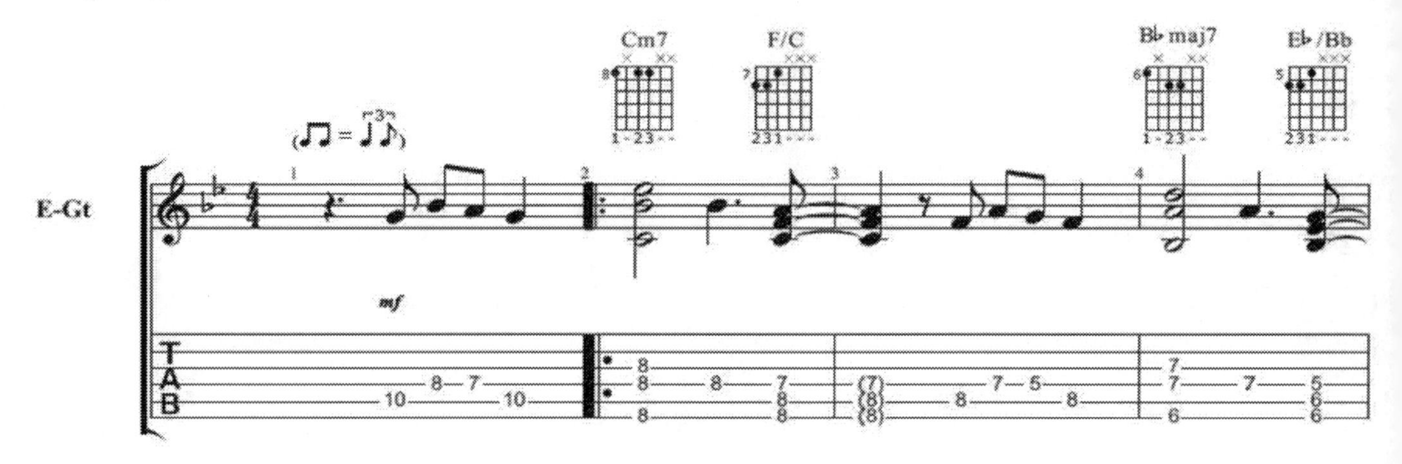

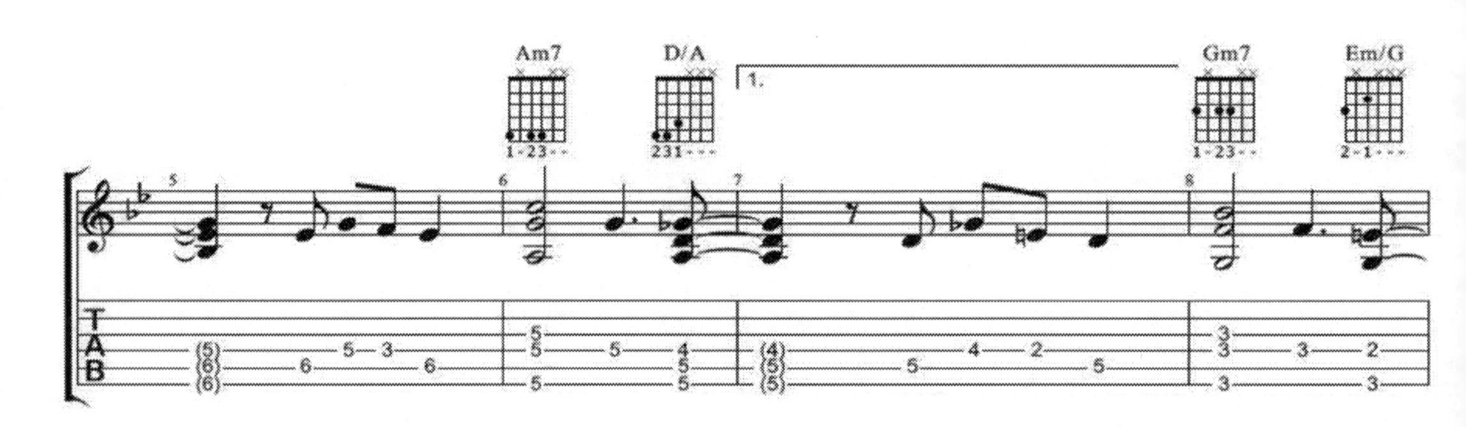

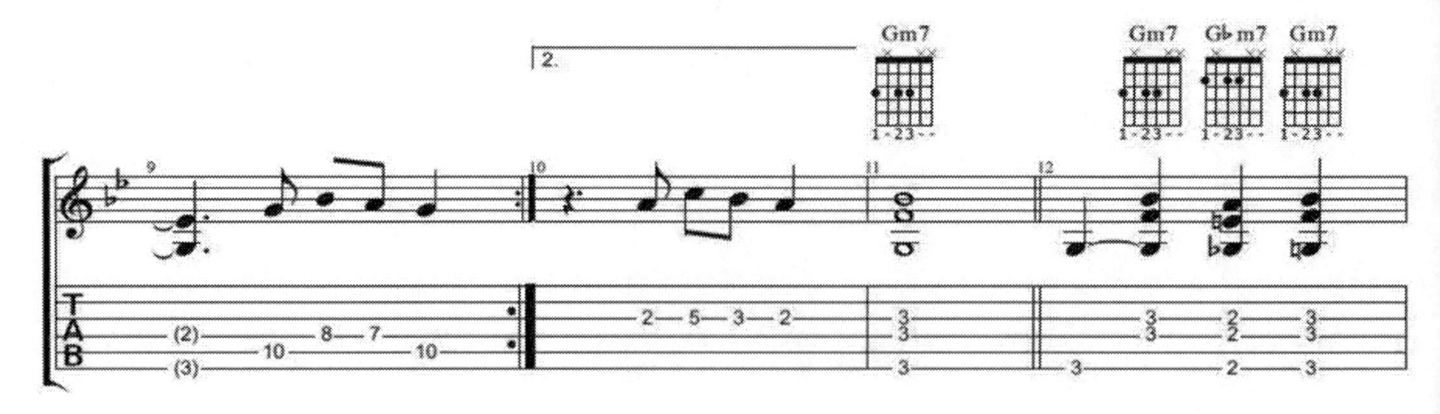

Am7
D7
Gm7
Gm7
Cm7
F7
F7
B♭maj7
E♭maj7
Am7
D7(♯9)
Gm7
C7
Fm7
B♭7
Am7
D7(♯9)
Gm7add11

Study #15

created ove "Bluesette" chord progression

study designed by Carlos Brizzola

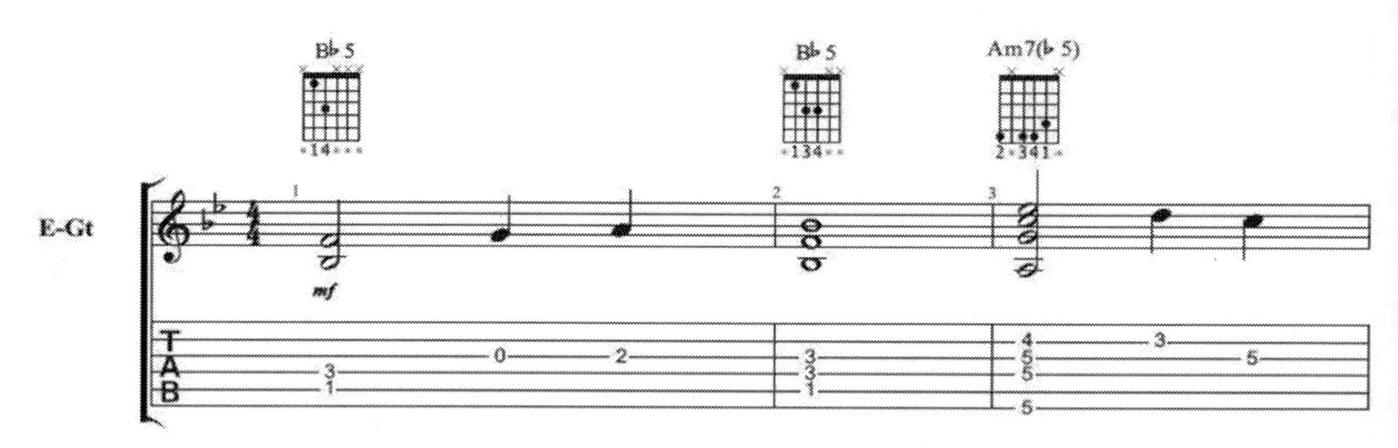

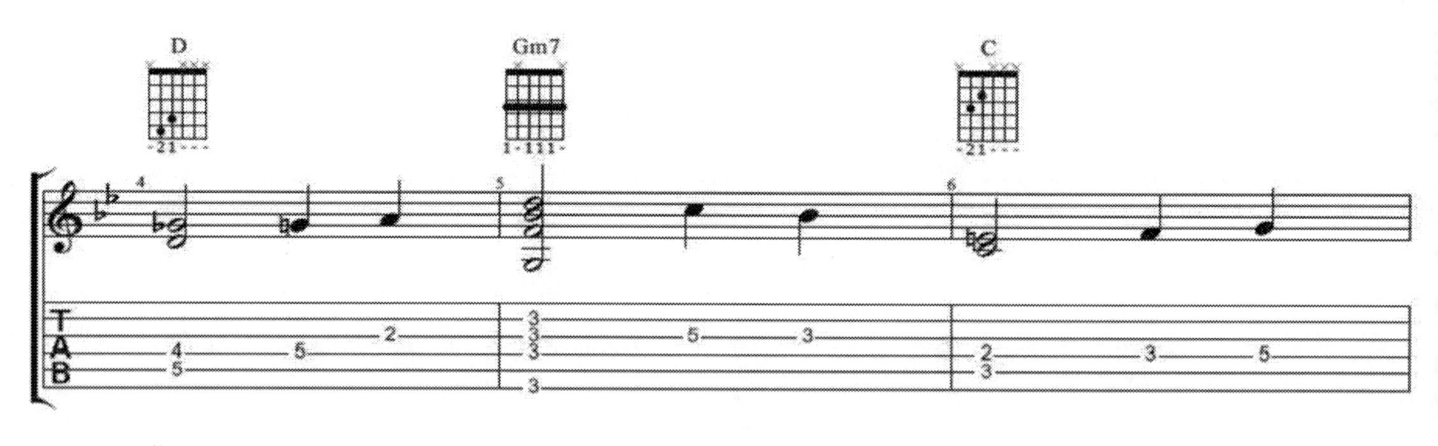

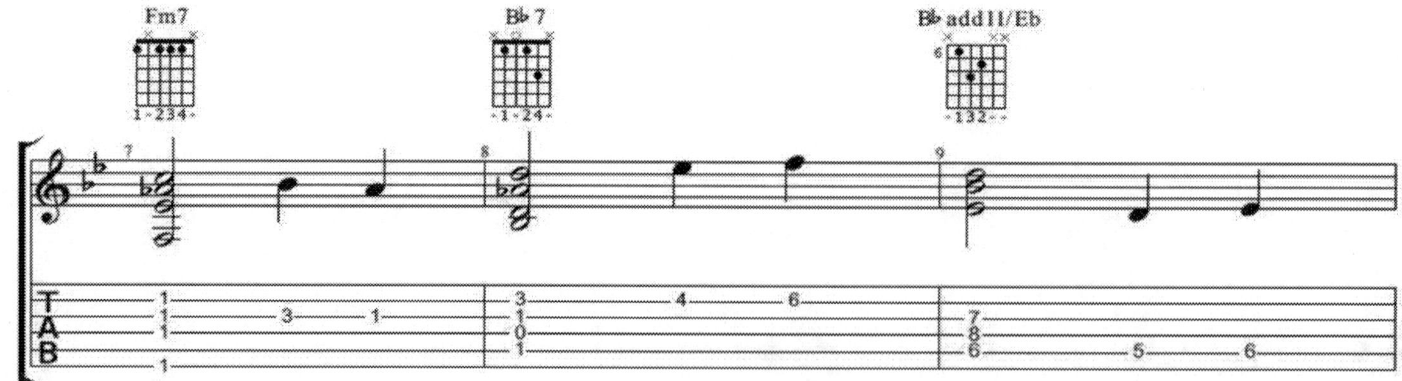

E♭m7
A♭7add13
D♭5
D♭maj7
A♭/D♭
D♭m7
G♭sus4
G♭
B5
B5
Cm7(11)
F6
Dm7

D♭7
Cm7
Faug/Eb
B♭maj7
E♭/F
G♭dim7
Gm7
Adim7
Bdim7
Cm7
Bdim7
D7
D7sus4
Gm7
C7
B♭/D
Em7(♭5)
Fm7
A♭sus2/F
B♭7
Fm/Bb
E♭maj7
E♭maj7sus4

Eb maj7
Bb /Eb
Eb m7
Fm7
Ab 7
Gb /Bb
Ab /C
Db maj7
Ab /Db
Db 5
Ab add11/Db
Bb m7/Db
Db m7
Gb 7sus4
Gb 7
B5
B5
Cm7add11
F6
Dm7

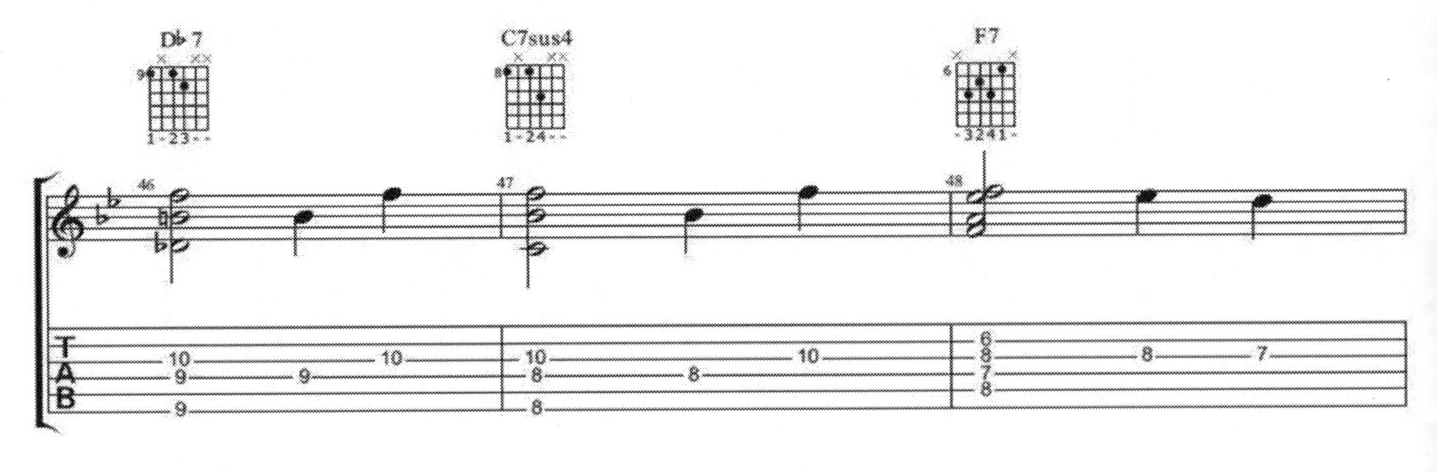
D♭7
C7sus4
F7

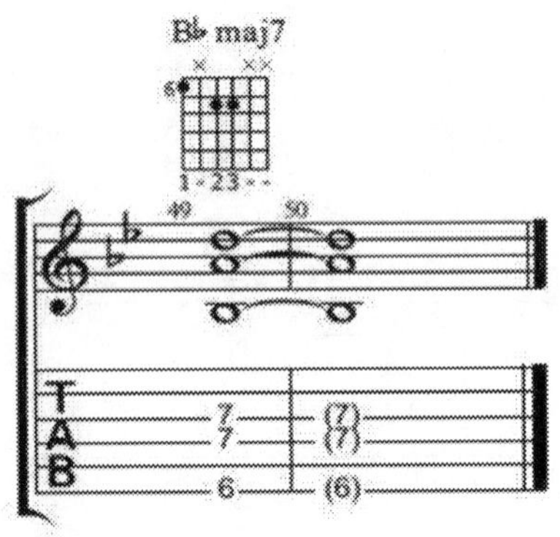
B♭maj7

Study #16

created over "Beautiful Love" chord progression

study designed by Carlos Brizzola

Standard tuning

 = 120

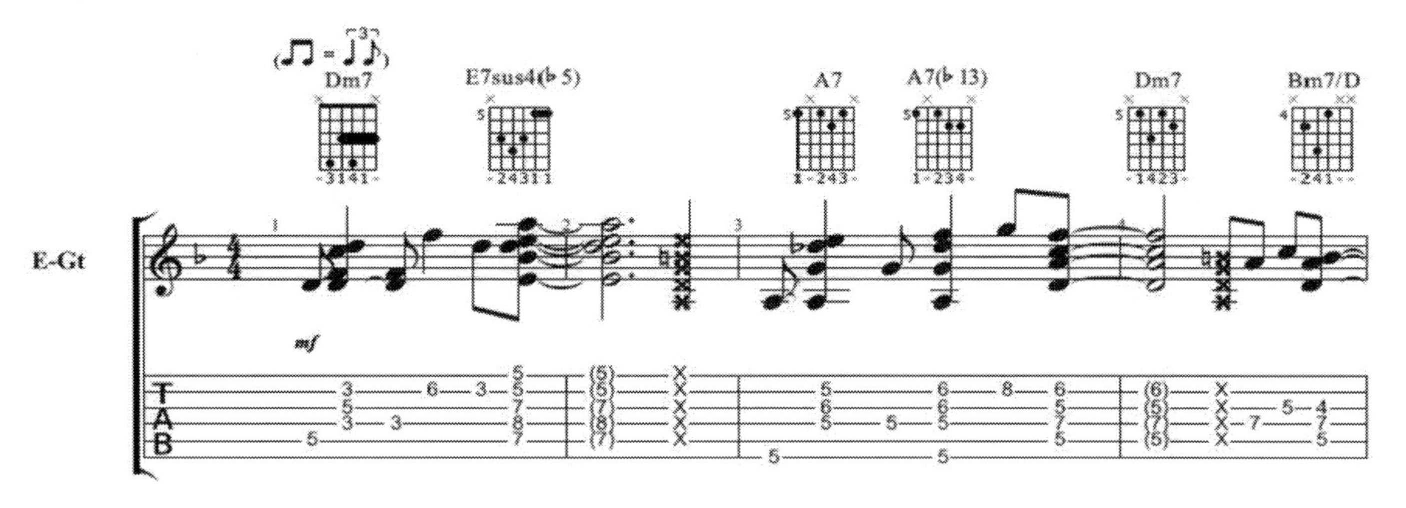

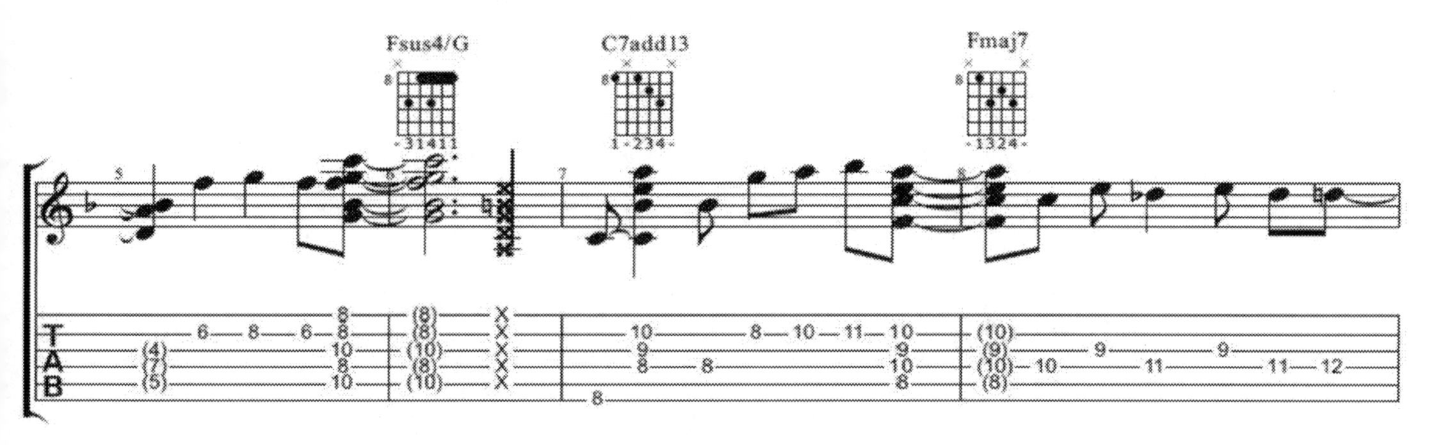

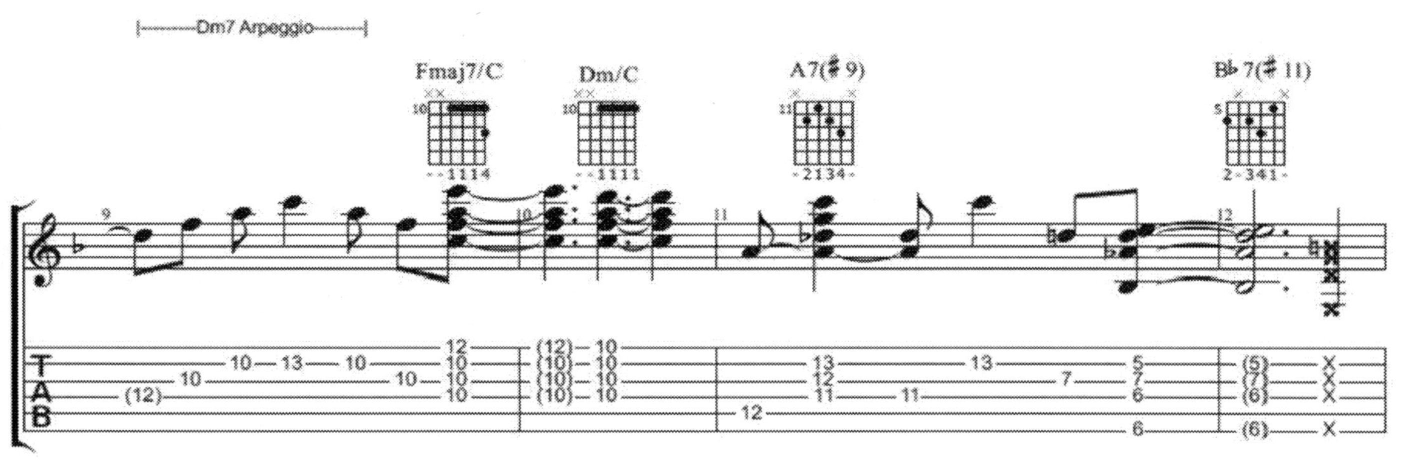

A7
A7(♭13)
Dm7
D♭aug/B
Dsus2(♯5)/E
A7
A7(♭13)
E7sus4(♭5)
A7
A7(♭13)
Dm7
Bm7/D
Fsus4/G
C7add13
Fmaj7
Fmaj7/C

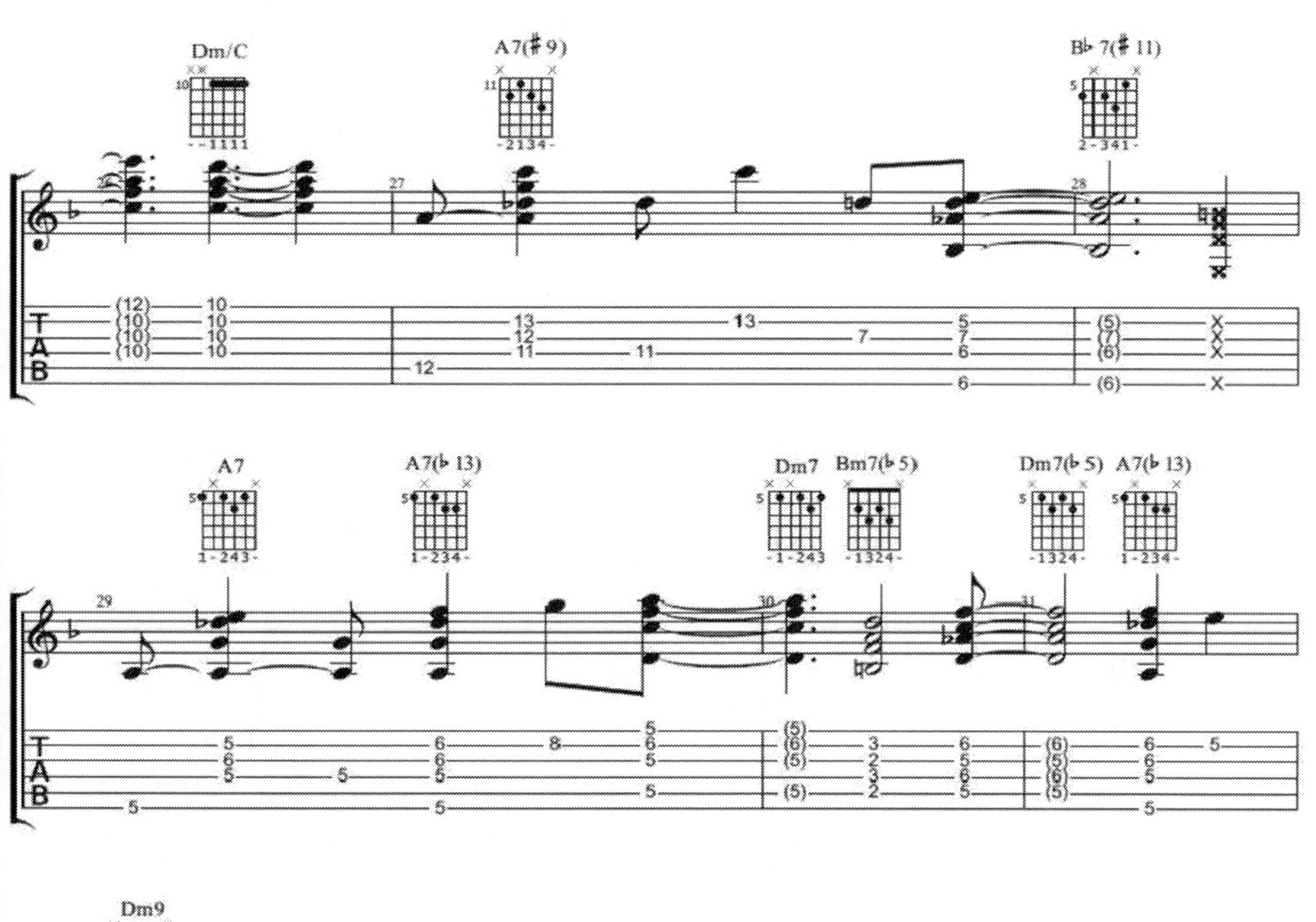
Dm/C
A7(♯9)
B♭7(♯11)
A7
A7(♭13)
Dm7
Bm7(♭5)
Dm7(♭5)
A7(♭13)

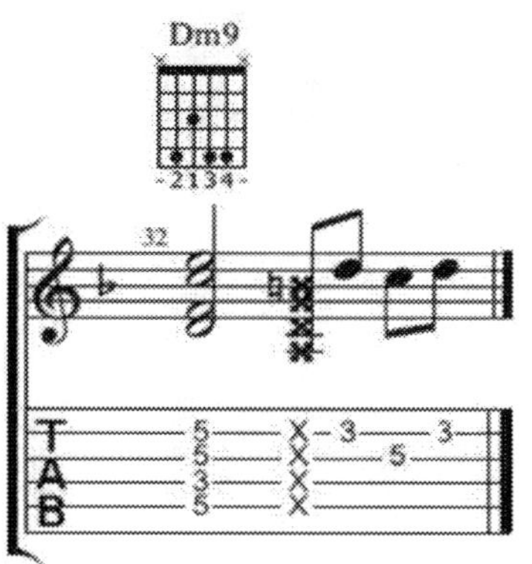
Dm9

About the Author

Jazz guitarist and arranger, Carlos Brizzola picked up the guitar very early in his life listening to Bossa Nova, Samba, Rock and Gospel Music. His love for Jazz was developed gradually, as he swiftly passed from Rock to Jazz-Rock and finally into Jazz.
As a music producer and arranger, he has developed and assisted in many musical projects ranging from Jazz Guitar, piano, bass, brass sections, saxophone and string instruments, as well as arranging for an entirely Jazz and Latin band. He also has performed live sessions on radio, TV and independent visual productions around Italy, Brazil and UK. Carlos graduated at London College of Music and Thames Valley University, and has a vast experience playing, teaching and arranging for his primary instrument, the Jazz Guitar. He currently teaches Music Composition & Arrangement, Music Technology, Music Production, Rehearsal Techniques and Music Theory, in Colleges around London and has done so for many years.

Printed in the United States
By Bookmasters